M

Rhode

Everything yo
Rhode Island and

Tim Lehnert

MACINTYRE PURCELL PUBLISHING INC.

974.5
Lehne.T

TO OUR READERS

Every effort has been made by authors and editors to ensure that the information enclosed in this book is accurate and up-to-date. We revise and update annually, however, many things can change after a book gets published. If you discover any out-of-date or incorrect information in Rhode Island 101, we would appreciate hearing from you via our website, **www.101bookseries.com**.

Copyright 2009 by MacIntyre Purcell Publishing Inc.

MacIntyre Purcell Publishing Inc.
232 Lincoln St., PO Box 1142
Lunenburg, Nova Scotia
B0J 2C0 Canada
www.101bookseries.com
info@101bookseries.com

Cover photo courtesy: Richard Benjamin
Inside images: iStock
Map courtesy: Rhode Island Department of Transportation
Design and layout: Channel Communications
Printed and bound in Canada by Friesens

Library and Archives Canada Cataloguing in Publication

Lehnert, Tim
    Rhode Island 101 / Tim Lehnert.

ISBN 978-0-9810941-0-6

        1. Rhode Island. 2. Rhode Island--Miscellanea. I. Title.
F77.3.L44 2009   974.5   C2008-905738-4

Introduction

The hardest part about putting *Rhode Island 101* together was deciding what not to include. We left a lot out, and aspects of Rhode Island which others have written entire books on were dispatched in but a single paragraph or short list. But that winnowing process was also part of the fun – figuring out how to distill a colorful, fascinating (and old) state into 248 pages.

One of the ways we got to the salty essence of the Ocean State was by asking 26 Rhody experts for their insight. Locals and expats will recognize such favorites as Lincoln Chafee, Michael Corrente, John Ghiorse, Charlie Hall, Mark Patinkin, Bruce Sundlun, Jim Taricani and Arlene Violet. Visitors might not know all of these names, but will still profit from getting the local low-down straight from some quintessential Rhode Islanders.

Rhode Island has an august history, and is a vital and diverse place, but in trying to put as much meaty clam into the stuffie as possible, we didn't shy away from less appealing parts of the state. In addition to that which makes Rhode Island great, we've included crime and economic decline, as well as the periodic bouts of political corruption and lousy weather that plague the state.

It was a lot of fun working on this project, so much so that I'd hardly call it work at all; although that's the story I kept telling my wife. She also had to endure many one-sided conversations of the "Did you know that Rhode Island . . ." variety. In addition to my wife, big thanks to fellow Cranstonian Steve Stycos for writing the bulk of the Politics, Natural World and Slang chapters, and to Rudy Cheeks for early consultations. Thanks also to Leita Adeymi, and to John MacIntyre and Kelly Inglis in the home office. Esteemed Rhode Islanders generously gave me lists of five on diverse topics including vampires, endangered animals, Providence architecture, ghosts and classic diners. I learned a lot. Finally, thanks to the many uncredited Ocean Staters who offered me valuable suggestions on what had to be included in this brief survey of a one-of-a-kind place.

Table of Contents

Rhode Island's It For Me

Lyrics by *Charlie Hall*
Music by *Maria Day*
Arranged by *Kathryn Chester*

I've been to every state we have
and I think that I'm inclined to say
that Rhody stole my heart:
You can keep the forty nine

Herring gulls that dot the sky,
blue waves that paint the rocks,
waters rich with Neptune's life,
the boats that line the docks,
I see the lighthouse flickering
to help the sailors see.
There's a place for everyone:
Rhode Island's it for me.

Rhode Island, oh, Rhode Island
surrounded by the sea.
Some people roam the earth for
home;
Rhode Island's it for me.

I love the fresh October days,
the buzz on College Hill,
art that moves an eye to tear,
a jeweler's special skill.
Icicles refract the sun,
snow falling gracefully.
Some search for a place that's
warm:
Rhode Island's it for me.

Rhode Island, oh, Rhode Island
surrounded by the sea.
Some people roam the earth for
home;
Rhode Island's it for me.

The skyline piercing
Providence,
the State House dome so rare,
residents who speak their minds;
No longer unaware!
Roger Williams would be proud
to see
his "colony"
so don't sell short this precious
port:
Rhode Island's it for me.

Rhode Island, oh, Rhode Island
surrounded by the sea.
Some people roam the earth for
home;
Rhode Island's it for me.

Rhode Island, oh, Rhode Island
surrounded by the sea.
Some people roam the earth for
home:
Rhode Island's it for me!

Rhode Island:

A Timeline

10,000 years ago: Native Americans inhabit the territory now known as Rhode Island.

1524: Giovanni da Verrazzano, exploring the Atlantic Coast on behalf of France, "discovers" Rhode Island.

1614: Adriaen Block, a Dutch mariner, visits Block Island and bestows his name upon it.

1620s: Massachusetts Bay and Plymouth Colony settlers visit and trade with Native peoples.

1635: Reverend William Blackstone becomes area's first European resident when he builds a house in what is now Cumberland.

1636: Roger Williams, a religious refugee from Massachusetts, establishes the first permanent European settlement in Rhode Island at Providence.

1638-42: The towns of Portsmouth, Newport and Warwick are founded. America's First Baptist Church is established in Providence. (The current building on North Main Street was completed in 1775).

1644: Roger Williams obtains first charter from England uniting Rhode Island.

1663: Royal Charter establishes the "Colony of Rhode Island and Providence Plantations." The Charter guarantees religious freedom and allows for substantial self-governance.

1675-76: King Philip's War devastates the Native population and results in Providence being burnt to the ground.

1700s: Rhode Island grows and prospers thanks to agriculture, fishing and the shipping industry. Newport, Bristol, and Providence are busy ports.

1763: Newport's Touro Synagogue, the first in North America, is dedicated.

1764: The College of Rhode Island, later renamed Brown University, is founded.

1760s-70s: Several incidents in which the Colonists rebel against the English, most famously the 1772 burning of the British ship *The Gaspee* after it runs aground in Warwick pursuing smugglers.

1772-82: Rhode Island loses nearly 10 percent of its population, the result of war casualties, Loyalists departing for England and Canada and a poor economy.

1775: A year after sending delegates to the Continental Congress, the General Assembly creates a 1,500 man army, the first permanent army in the colonies.

1776: On May 4, Rhode Island becomes the first colony to declare independence from Great Britain. Aquidneck Island is occupied by the British in December.

1778: The Battle of Rhode Island, the only full blown Revolutionary era battle on Rhode Island soil, takes place. American troops, initially helped by the French, attack British forces occupying Newport. The Black Regiment, a battalion of black soldiers, assists the Americans who ultimately are forced to retreat. British forces quit Newport the following year.

1784: Slavery is abolished by the General Assembly by virtue of the "Gradual Emancipation Act."

1787: The Constitutional Convention is held in Philadelphia; Rhode Island is the only future US state not to send delegates.

1790: Rhode Island is the last of the original thirteen colonies to rat-ify the US Constitution with the condition that a Bill of Rights be included.

1790-93: America's Industrial Revolution begins on the banks of the Blackstone River in Pawtucket when Samuel Slater builds the United States' first cotton mill.

1800: Providence surpasses Newport as Rhode Island's largest city.

1815: The "Great Gale" causes serious damage.

1820s: Rhode Island rapidly industrializes and the Blackstone River Valley becomes a world center for textile production.

Bio Roger Williams

Rhode Island's founder, Roger Williams, is famous for his belief that religion is a matter of individual conscience. This radical idea became enshrined in the First Amendment to the US Constitution, 150 years after Williams championed it.

Williams was born in London in 1603 and was a brilliant scholar who graduated from Cambridge University. He was friends with John Milton, whom he taught Dutch in exchange for Hebrew lessons. Williams became a Puritan minister, but was unable to abide the prevailing Anglican orthodoxy, and quit England with his wife Mary. They arrived in the Massachusetts Bay Colony in 1631, and Williams soon got into trouble. He offended local clergy with his views on religious freedom, and furthermore opined that it was the Natives who actually owned the land, not the Colonists.

Williams fled Massachusetts in 1635 under threat of arrest and deportation. He went south in the dead of winter, finding shelter with Indian chiefs Massasoit and Canonicus, and founding Providence in 1636 on land bought from the Narragansett Indians. Rather than trying to subjugate the Natives, Williams spent time among them learning their languages and customs.

In 1644, Williams obtained a charter from England to unite the territory's settlements and protect them against attack from neighboring colonies. A Royal Charter establishing "Rhode Island and Providence Plantations" followed in 1663; it further enshrined religious freedom and allowed for the election of governor and other offices. Quakers, Jews, and Baptists found sanctuary in Rhode Island, which became known as "Rogue's Island" for its reputation for taking in cast-offs and undesirables.

If the 1663 charter was a high point, the events of 1675-76 represented a low ebb for Williams, as Providence was burned during King Philip's War. Williams died in 1683, the father of six children, one of whom was named "Providence." His remains are interred beneath a monument to him that was created in the 1930s and installed in Prospect Terrace Park on Providence's East Side. The 35-foot stone Williams figure is a few blocks from America's First Baptist Church, which he founded in 1638, and looks down over the city he established in 1636.

They said it

"Forced worship stinks in God's nostrils."
— **Roger Williams in a 1670 letter.**

1828: Blackstone Canal, linking Worcester, MA and Providence, opens; it closes in 1848. School Act establishes free public education.

1829: The *Providence Journal*, the oldest continually publishing daily in North America, debuts.

1831: Race riot in Providence produces five deaths and prompts the city to incorporate the following year.

1835: Railroad connecting Providence and Boston begins operation.

1839: Kingscote, the first of the Newport Mansions, is commissioned.

1842: Dorr's Rebellion expands the franchise and increases the power of non-property owners and urban dwellers. State constitution is adopted.

1846: Providence and Worcester Railroad debuts; Providence's Union Station opens two years later.

1860: Rhode Island is the most industrialized state in the country with half of its workforce employed in manufacturing. Child labor is common.

1860s: Rhode Island sends over 25,000 soldiers to fight on behalf of the Union effort in the Civil War. Local factories supply weapons, munitions, uniforms and other manufactured goods.

TAKE 5 TED WIDMER'S FIVE WAYS
RHODE ISLAND INFLUENCED THE UNITED STATES

Ted Widmer directs the John Carter Brown Library at Brown University, a leading center for research on early American history. Raised in Providence, he was educated at Harvard University and is author of *Martin Van Buren* (2005), *Campaigns: A Century of Presidential Races* (with Alan Brinkley, 2001), and *Young America: The Flowering of Democracy in New York City* (1999). A former speech writer and advisor to President Clinton, Widmer frequently contributes essays on American history and foreign policy to the *New York Times*, the *Washington Post* and the *Los Angeles Times*.

1. **Shockingly Decent Treatment of Natives.** From the moment in 1636 when Roger Williams set foot on what was to become Providence, he established fair and honest relations with the native peoples living in the region. This may perhaps have stemmed from pure realism – after all, he was considerably outnumbered, and had nowhere to return to. But it also came from principle – Williams had advocated for the rights of natives in Massachusetts, one of the reasons he was unceremoniously booted, and his first book, *A Key into the Language of America* (1643), celebrated many aspects of native life. Not all Rhode Islanders have lived up to his high standards – as we continue to learn, Rhode Island merchants were active in the slave trade, to cite one of many imperfections afflicting our nearly perfect state. But still, he set the bar high.

2. **Religious Toleration.** One of America's most sacred ideas is that we can worship whatever deity we choose, on whatever day we want, wearing whatever ceremonial outfit pleases us. That owes more than a little to Rhode Island, which was light years ahead of the rest of New England, and preeminent in America as well. In Rhode Island, the pursuit of "soul liberty" was a clearly articulated ideal from the beginning and went beyond Christianity as Williams said that in theory Jews and Muslims would be welcome. The tradition was given a strong boost when George Washington came to Newport in 1790, visited Touro Synagogue, and wrote an exquisite letter in praise of religious diversity.

3. **Independence.** On May 4, 1776, Rhode Island voted to withdraw its allegiance to King George III, which in a sense made this tiny colony a free entity two months before the Declaration of Independence created the United States. That certainly would have happened anyway, but Rhode Island's brave act was a significant step on the way to nationhood, tarnishing the aura of the British crown, and showing that courageous statesmen could chart their own destiny.

4. **The Bill of Rights.** This great charter of human rights was ratified in 1791 and owes more than a little to Little Rhody. Rhode Island's independent streak also stood out during the difficult first years following the drafting of the Constitution in 1787. Rhode Islanders refused to attend the convention that drafted the document (they were eternally suspicious of central authority), and refused to ratify it until 1790, more than a year after Washington became president. Once again, this was a state without a country, and one of the means used to induce Rhode Islanders to join the other twelve states was a promise that rights would be enumerated publicly. The first amendment, promising freedom of religion, seems tailor-made for Rhode Islanders.

5. **Prosperity.** It feels a little odd, after listing all of the ways in which Rhode Islanders advanced the notion of rights, to remember that the Industrial Revolution also began here. In 1793, only three years after Rhode Island joined the US, Slater Mill was built in Pawtucket. Soon factories dotted Rhode Island's river valleys, from Woonsocket to West Warwick. At first they were small and quaint, as Slater Mill remains, but they grew much larger, and as they prospered, labor conditions did not always keep pace. Children worked in mills in the early years, and women and immigrants later toiled long hours without many protections. But the factories prospered, and economic self-sufficiency was a critical source of strength for the shaky republic. The profits made in Rhode Island allowed many other industries to develop, from machine parts and tools to steam engines, and there was hardly a business in America that did not have some connection to Rhode Island.

King Philip's War

King Philip's War was a 15-month conflict fought in 1675-76 which ended any hopes Natives might have had of either vanquishing the Europeans, or co-existing with them on an even footing.

Life around Narragansett Bay in the 1670s was complex. In addition to the Rhode Island colony, there were Wampanoag, Narragansett and other Indian tribes, as well as the nearby Massachusetts Bay and Plymouth colonies.

Wampanoag Chief Massasoit had long been a friend to Roger Williams and other colonists. However, Massasoit died in 1661, and his son, Metacomet (aka King Philip), became disenchanted with the steady loss of Wampanoag lands to the Plymouth Colony, as well as the increasing subjugation of the Wampanoag people at the hands of the Puritans.

The conflict began with a June 1675 Wampanoag raid on Swansea (then a part of Plymouth Colony). Clashes continued for months, and the Narragansett provided refuge for many Wampanoag in a fortified settlement surrounded by swamp in what is now South Kingstown. In December 1675, over 1,000 soldiers from the Plymouth, Massachusetts and Connecticut colonies attacked this encampment, battling Narragansett warriors and burning dwellings, killing hundreds of women and children. This siege came to be known as the "Great Swamp Fight," and it was just one episode in an ongoing war that caused most white settlers to flee mainland Rhode Island.

In March 1676, the Narragansett, under Chief Canonchet, killed a force of 55 Plymouth soldiers sent to Central Falls. They then burned Providence, but spared Roger Williams personally. Violence spread throughout New England, but in less than a year the European settlers were victorious. In April 1676, Canonchet was executed, and in August, Metacomet was killed near Bristol and his wife and nine-year-old son sold into slavery. Ultimately, many of the captured Natives were sent to the Caribbean to work as slaves, or wound up as indentured servants locally. The Narragansett merged with the Niantics, and were limited to 18,000 acres in Charlestown. In the conflict's aftermath, Rhode Island's white population lived almost exclusively on Aquidneck Island, and Newport became the colony's principal town.

They said it

"Thus tract after tract is gone. But a small part of the dominions of my ancestors remain. I am determined not to live until I have no country."

— **Wampanoag Chief Metacomet, also known as King Philip, 1670s.**

1863: Rhode Island Hospital is founded.

1866: Racial segregation is outlawed.

1882: Public schooling becomes mandatory.

1883-84: Newport Naval Station and US Naval War College open.

1884: The Providence Grays defeat the New York Metropolitans in the first World Series.

1880s-1920: Substantial immigration from Quebec, the British Isles and northern and southern Europe changes the face of the state.

1895: The Breakers, the most extravagant of the Newport Mansions, is completed.

1900-01: Providence becomes Rhode Island's only capital (previously it shared this role with Newport). The new State House opens for business.

1905: Rhode Island becomes a majority Catholic state.

1917: The US enters WWI and over 28,000 Rhode Islanders join the army. Women gain the right to vote.

1920s-30s: Massive decline in the textile industry due to relocation to the southern states and the Depression.

1922: 600-room Biltmore Hotel opens in Providence; local radio stations begin broadcasting.

Slavery

The first Rhode Island slave ships set out in the early 1700s, and by the 1720s Rhode Island was a well established slave trading center. Slavery would be a notable part of the Rhode Island economy into the nineteenth century. Using Narragansett Bay's harbors and ships, many Rhode Islanders became rich through the "Triangle Trade." Wealthy businessmen, including the DeWolf family and John Brown, sent ships laden with rum to Africa to purchase slaves. Chained and packed into ship hulls, the Africans were brought to Caribbean sugar plantations and sold for molasses or sugar. The ships then journeyed to Bristol, Newport, or Providence with sugar for local rum distilleries.

By 1750, Rhode Island had 33 distilleries, and by 1755 almost 5,000 slaves, primarily on South County farms. Subsequently, Quakers, then Congregationalists and Baptists, freed their slaves and campaigned to end the practice. Moses Brown freed his ten slaves in 1773, but his brother John continued to sell Africans for decades. Moses Brown's Abolition Society even led the 1797 prosecution against John Brown for slave trading.

During the mid and late 1700s, there were many enslaved African Americans, but also free Blacks, some of whom were skilled craftsmen and sailors. During the American Revolution, soldiers were needed to fight the British, and the colony purchased slaves from their owners to use as conscripts, freeing them at the end of their service. In 1784, Rhode Island declared future children born of slave mothers free upon their 21st birthday. A 1787 law prohibited Rhode Islanders from participating in slavery, although the financing of the slave trade continued for some time. The state's last remaining slave died in 1859.

1926: Scituate Reservoir begins operation, capping a decade long construction project.

1929: Mount Hope Bridge connecting Bristol and Portsmouth replaces the ferry.

1931: Hillsgrove State Airport opens in Warwick; it is renamed T.F. Green State Airport after the former governor in 1938.

1935: "Bloodless Revolution" changes state politics and shifts power to the Democrats.

1936: Rhode Island celebrates its 300th birthday.

1938: A major hurricane causes over 250 deaths and alters the state's coastline.

1940: Jamestown Bridge links Conanicut Island with the mainland.

1941-45: Over 92,000 Rhode Islanders serve during WWII; thousands more on the home front are engaged in wartime production.

1950s-60s: Movement of population to suburbs; Providence shrinks dramatically.

1953: Senator John F. Kennedy is married to Jacqueline Bouvier at St. Mary's Church in Newport.

1954: First Newport Jazz Festival (the folk festival debuts in 1959). Hurricane Carol hits at the end of August, causing major damage.

1966: Route 95 is completed through the length of Rhode Island.

TAKE 5 RORY RAVEN'S TOP FIVE
TALES OF HAUNTED RHODE ISLAND

Providence mentalist and mind bender Rory Raven appears at colleges, clubs, theatres, festivals and private events entertaining audiences with his paranormal skills. An expert in the "Theatre of the Mind," Raven also conducts the Providence Ghost Walk, and is the author of the 2008 book *Haunted Providence: Strange Tales from the Smallest State*.

1. **Mercy Brown**. Mercy Brown died of tuberculosis in 1892 at the tender age of 19. After her death, rumors began to circulate that she was a vampire, especially once her brother Edwin fell ill with the same disease. Following a bizarre folk medicine procedure, Mercy Brown's body was exhumed and examined. According to legend, she had rolled over in her coffin. Mercy's heart was removed and burned, and the ashes were mixed with water and given to Edwin to drink. This was supposed to cure him, but Edwin died a few months later.
Mercy Brown is THE Rhode Island Hallowe'en story.

2. **Ramtail Mill**. This cotton mill stood in the woods near Foster for a number of years, patrolled by its night watchman, Peleg Walker. After a fierce argument with the owners, Peleg hanged himself, and it is said that his restless spirit continued making nightly rounds. Strange things began happening, including machinery starting on its own and the mill bell ringing in the middle of the night. Some reported seeing Peleg's lantern shining through the building's windows. The mill was eventually abandoned and stood empty for a number of years. In the 1885 census, the mill was described as "haunted," making it Rhode Island's only "official" haunt. The mill is long gone, but the stories remain.

3. **Palatine Light.** A passenger ship making its way from Holland to Philadelphia was blown off course and made landfall on the north side of Block Island. According to the most popular version of the legend, a

gang of pirates called the Block Island Wreckers lured the ship onto the rocks by lighting false beacons, then looted the helpless vessel and robbed the passengers. The Wreckers set the boat on fire, and it was then carried away by the rising tide. One woman, who had lost her mind during the voyage, would not leave the vessel, and her screams were heard as the ship vanished over the horizon.

Every year in December, a flaming ship appears off the north shore of Block Island, and the shrieks of a burning madwoman may be heard.

4. **Benefit Street.** Often called the most haunted street in the state, Benefit Street is home to many ghost stories and weird tales. Edgar Allan Poe courted fellow poet Sarah Helen Whitman at her home and at the Athenaeum, both on Benefit. Some say Poe still walks the street in the dead of night. Horror writer H. P. Lovecraft also roamed the neighborhood, even writing the 1924 short story "The Shunned House" about one of the allegedly haunted homes there. Benefit is as strange as it is picturesque.

5. **The Old Rhode Island Statehouse.** The Old Statehouse at 150 Benefit Street, which dates from 1762, was the scene of a notorious murder trial in the 1840s. John Gordon, a recent Irish immigrant, stood accused of murdering Amassa Sprague, a wealthy and prosperous mill owner from Cranston. The trial caused a sensation and was the most talked-about event of the day. John Gordon was found guilty and hanged. After the trial, however, new evidence was uncovered and new witnesses came forward, clearing Gordon's name. The identity of the real murderer remains unknown to this day. John Gordon's restless spirit has been said to haunt the building where he was tried and unjustly convicted so many years ago.

TAKE 5 MICHAEL CORRENTE'S TOP FIVE
RHODE ISLAND SUBJECTS FOR BIOPICS

Michael Corrente was raised in Pawtucket and Coventry, where he moved at age 14. A graduate of Coventry High, Corrente studied at Providence's Trinity Repertory Conservatory, and then moved to New York where he was a prolific playwright. His first film, *Federal Hill*, was based on one of his plays. Since this 1993 debut, Corrente has served as writer, director or producer on many movies, including several with connections to his home state. Corrente directed *Outside Providence*, on which he collaborated with fellow Rhode Islanders Peter and Bobby Farrelly, and which was filmed in a number of locations throughout Rhode Island. He also served as director on *American Buffalo*, which was shot in Pawtucket. Most recently, Corrente is producer and director of *The Prince of Providence*, a feature film about Buddy Cianci based on *Providence Journal* writer Mike Stanton's book of the same name.

1. **Vincent "Buddy" Cianci (1941-)**. Nuff said.

2. **Vinny Paz (1962-)**. One of only two pro fighters in the history of boxing to capture world championships as a lightweight and a middle weight. The Cranston-raised Paz achieved this feat after rehabbing from a broken neck sustained in a car accident.

3. **H.P. Lovecraft (1890-1937)**. The godfather of the horror genre. Steven King has dubbed Lovecraft "the twentieth century's greatest practitioner of the classic horror tale." All that creepiness was spawned right on Angell Street on Providence's East Side.

4. **Roger Williams (1603-1683)**. Roger did it his way centuries before Sinatra. Rhode Island's founder turned his back on the English church, and set sail for the New World, setting up shop to practice the religion he chose, where nobody could tell him what to do. It's an attitude that still resonates amongst Rhode Islanders.

5. **General Ambrose Burnside (1824-1881)**. An American soldier, railroad executive, inventor, industrialist, politician, and commander of the Union Army at the start of the Civil War. Sure he goes down in history as one of the worst military leaders ever, but there's no denying that his distinctive style of facial hair led to the term "sideburns". The Indiana-born Burnside was elected governor of Rhode Island three times, and also served as a US Senator from Rhode Island. He died in Bristol.

1968: Midland Mall, subsequently renamed Rhode Island Mall, opens. Warwick Malls follows four year later.

1969: Newport Bridge opens.

1972: Providence Civic Center opens.

1978: A blizzard drops several feet of snow and paralyzes much of the state for a week.

1989: A Greek tanker runs aground and spills 300,000 gallons of heating oil in Narragansett Bay. Seven years later, another accident results in a North Cape oil barge dropping 820,000 gallons of oil in the Bay.

1991: Governor Bruce Sundlun closes dozens of financial institutions in wake of the failure of the Rhode Island Share and Deposit Indemnity Corporation.

1990s: Providence Renaissance brings new life to downtown and includes uncovering the Providence River, and the opening of the Rhode Island Convention Center and Providence Place Mall.

2002: Providence Mayor Buddy Cianci resigns and reports to federal prison following conviction on corruption charges.

2003: Station Night Club fire in West Warwick kills 100 and seriously injures many others. In July, State Police raid a smoke-shop opened by Narragansett Indians on tribal land in Charlestown, seizing cigarettes and arresting tribe members including Chief Sachem Matthew Thomas.

2008-: Rhode Island endures one of its toughest economic troughs yet with high unemployment and gaping state budget deficits.

Rhode Island Essentials

WHAT'S IN A NAME

The state's official moniker is "Rhode Island and Providence Plantations," which is the longest name of any state in the union. The name is a bit of a puzzler as the pocket-sized land mass that comprises much of the state is not in fact an island.

One explanation is related to Giovanni da Verrazzano's 1524 visit to Narragansett Bay. Verrazzano, an Italian exploring the Atlantic Coast on behalf of France, spied what is now called Block Island and thought it similar in appearance to the Greek island of Rhodes and so bestowed the name "Rhode Island" upon it. Later, English colonists, perhaps out of confusion, applied this name to Aquidneck Island which is larger and much closer to the mainland.

Another version of the story holds that the "Rhode" name may have come from the 1614 voyage of Dutch explorer Adrian Block, who not only named Block Island after himself, but applied the name "roode" (Dutch for red) to Aquidneck.

Regardless of its provenance, the name was cemented when England's King Charles II granted the 1663 Royal Charter to the "Colony of Rhode Island and Providence Plantations." Recently, the "Providence Plantations" part of the name, which technically refers to the state's mainland, has generated controversy. Some Rhode

Islanders, particularly those of African descent, find the word "Plantations" racist, and would like to see the state's official name shortened to the commonly used "Rhode Island."

Location: One of the six New England states, Rhode Island is bordered on the north and east by Massachusetts, on the south by the Atlantic Ocean and on the west by Connecticut.

State capital: Providence

Motto: "Hope"

Nicknames: The "Ocean State" and "Little Rhody"

State seal: The seal features an anchor and the word "Hope" surrounded by the words "Seal of the State of Rhode Island and Providence Plantations, 1636."

State flag: The flag's background is white and features a circle of thirteen gold stars at its center. In the middle of the circle lies a gold anchor with a blue ribbon below it inscribed with the word "Hope."

Year of entry into the Union: 1790

Time zone: Eastern Standard Time

Area code: 401

Voting age: 18

Drinking age: 21

Zip codes: 91 zip codes, all beginning with "028" or "029."

Legal holidays: New Year's Day (January 1), Memorial Day (last Monday in May), Independence Day (July 4), Victory Day (second Monday in August), Labor Day (first Monday in September), Columbus Day (second Monday in October), Veteran's Day (November 11), Thanksgiving Day (fourth Thursday in November), and Christmas Day (December 25).

License plate: "Ocean State" appears at the bottom, and "Rhode Island" is along the top with a small anchor at the top left. The plate number is superimposed over a wave motif. Specialty plates include designations for war veterans, Purple Heart recipients, National Guard members, and firefighters. There are also specialty plates featuring a sailboat design, Mr. Potato Head (benefits the Rhode Island Community Food Bank), and Conservation Through Education (benefits Save the Bay and the Audubon Society of Rhode Island).

State quarter: Issued in 2001, it reads "Rhode Island 1790 The Ocean State" and features a vintage sailboat in the foreground, and the Claiborne Pell Newport Bridge in the background.

POPULATION

Rhode Island's population was estimated at 1,050,788 in July 2008. Among the six New England states, Rhode Island ranks fifth in population, ahead of Vermont which has about 621,000 people, and behind New Hampshire and Maine which have roughly 1.3 million people each.

Rhode Island is the 43rd most populous state in the US; Hawaii is number 42 and Montana number 44. Other places with a population comparable to Rhode Island's include the Caribbean nation of Trinidad and Tobago, and the western Canadian province of Saskatchewan. Rhode Island's largest city is Providence with a population of 172,459, ranking it 131st in the nation. The population of the Providence-New Bedford-Fall River RI-MA metropolitan statistical area is 1,600,856, ranking 36th in the nation.

- Rhode Island's percentage of the US population of 304.1 million: 0.035
- California's percentage of the US population: 12.1
- Rhode Island's percentage of New England's population: 7.3

Source: US Census Bureau.

COUNTIES

Rhode Island has five counties, and contrary to popular belief there is no such official entity as "South County"; South County Beaches are actually located in Washington County. Almost two-thirds of Rhode Island's population lives in Providence County, which in addition to the city of Providence includes the municipalities of Woonsocket, Cumberland, Pawtucket, East Providence, North Providence, Johnston and Cranston.

TAKE 5 — MARK PATINKIN'S TOP FIVE SIGNS YOU'VE BEEN IN RHODE ISLAND TOO LONG

Mark Patinkin grew up in Chicago, but has lived in Rhode Island for more than 30 years. His syndicated column appears in the *Providence Journal* three times weekly, and he is author of *The Rhode Island Dictionary* and *Up and Running: The Inspiring True Story of a Boy's Struggle to Survive and Triumph*. Patinkin lives in Providence with his wife and three children.

1. You stop using turning signals.
2. You haven't gone to a restaurant that's more than 10 minutes away in two years.
3. You get a vanity plate.
4. You start planning your retirement in "Flahrider."
5. You start giving directions by landmark instead of street name: "And then you go under the overpass they tore down 10 years ago...."

County	Pop in thousands	County Seat or Courthouse
Providence	629.4	Providence
Kent	168.6	East Greenwich
Washington	126.9	West Kingston
Newport	82.8	Newport
Bristol	50.1	Bristol

Source: US Census Bureau.

SMALL, BUT DENSE

At 1,045 square miles of land, Rhode Island is the smallest state in the union. Number 49 ranked Delaware is about twice as big, and the city of Houston, Texas is a little more than half Little Rhody's size. Rhode Island's diminutive footprint results in its invocation as a unit of measurement for everything from icebergs, fires, and oil spills to western cattle ranches and foreign principalities. Whether describing an ice shelf or European duchy as "half the size of Rhode Island" clarifies matters is another story.

Moreover, there is no agreement on Rhode Island's size — it is variously reported as just over 1,000 square miles (US Census Bureau), approximately 1,200 square miles (State of Rhode Island) and over 1,500 square miles (World Almanac). It all depends on whether inland and Narragansett Bay water is included. Regardless, Rhode Island's 39 cities and towns are crammed into a limited space, making the state the second most densely populated in the country, trailing only New Jersey.

They said it

". . . Rhode Island's biggest tourist attraction is not so much its glittering coastline, but its seedy gothic heart . . ."

– Penelope Green, *New York Times*, 2001.

You Know You're From

- You think imprisonment is a standard part of a politician's career path.

- You feel a twinge of pride when you see an Ocean State Job Lot store while vacationing in New Hampshire.

- Employees at multiple Dunkin' Donuts franchises greet you by name and know your "reguluh."

- You don't consider Brown University (unlike RIC, URI and PC) a true Rhode Island school.

- You own a commemorative plate of either JFK & Jackie, Frank Sinatra, or a Pope.

- You can think of no greater honor than having a low-numbered license plate.

- A coffee table fashioned from a wooden lobster trap is in your Florida room or parlor.

- You pronounce "Woonasquatucket" fearlessly.

- You think "a couple of cases of beer" is suitable payment for any favor, from plant watering to bid rigging.

- You shudder at the memory of white knuckle car trips looking down at the grates on the old Jamestown Bridge, certain you would never make it to the other side.

- You have a cache of swizzle sticks and matchbooks from Twin Oaks and other "special occasion" Rhode Island eateries.

- Rocks and sea glass gathered from South County beaches adorn your mantel piece.

- Your children attend the same elementary school as you did.

- You've bet on Newport jai alai players and Lincoln dogs, even though you suspected that both were fixed.

- You've argued about whether the thing on the Federal Hill arch is a pignoli producing pinecone, or a pineapple.

Rhode Island When . . .

- You think of Foster as "out west."

- You can't park in your garage because a boat resting on ciderblocks is in the driveway.

- Your family is split on whether the Cardi Brothers are loveable or scary.

- You think crossing the bridge on I-195 linking downtown Providence to East Providence constitutes a major outing.

- Your children are (or were) Feinstein Jr. Scholars.

- You keep meaning, one of these days, to get to the Newport Jazz or Folk festival.

- You think the ultimate hockey franchise is the Mount Saint Charles Academy Mounties.

- You think there is no treasure so rare that it can't be obtained on Route 2 in Warwick.

- You'll drive five miles out of your way to save a quarter on a tank of gas, but spend ten minutes idling in the Dunkin' Donuts drive-thru.

- You know the path to the State House: LaSalle Academy, Providence College, Suffolk University Law School.

- You decide the governor and Congressional delegation are out of touch if you haven't bumped into them within the last month.

- You're on a first name basis with the mayor of your town because you (or your cousin, neighbor or aunt) went to school with his sister.

- You think everyone is Catholic.

- Your ears prick up when you hear Rhode Island mentioned in the national media, but you stop listening when you realize it's only because it's being used as a unit of measurement.

POPULATION DENSITIES PER SQUARE MILE

Wyoming	5
Massachusetts	816
Rhode Island	**1,029**
New Jersey	1,175
United States	84
Mexico	145
Netherlands	1,259
Providence	**9,400**
Central Falls, RI	**15,652**
New York City	27,281
Tokyo	33,617

TAKE 5 TOP FIVE RHODE ISLAND SYMBOLS

1. **An Anchor.** The anchor is the state's most prevalent official symbol; it was first adopted as colonial seal in 1647.

2. **Rhode Island Red chicken.** The Rhode Island Red originated in the 1850s when a domestic chicken was bred with an Asian rooster. It is considered an outstanding egg layer and was named the state bird in 1954.

3. **The Independent Man.** The 500-pound 11-foot tall gold plated Independent Man sits atop the State House and represents independence and freedom.

4. **Mr. Potato Head.** A 1952 creation of Pawtucket's Hasbro Inc., Mr. Potato Head has been widely licensed and is much beloved in his home state.

5. **The Big Blue Bug.** The 58-foot long nine-foot tall termite is a familiar sight to anyone who has driven I-95 south of downtown Providence. The bug, the mascot for New England Pest Control, debuted in 1980 and has been featured on state lottery tickets and in the movie *Dumb & Dumber*.

CRADLE TO GRAVE
Births: 12,687
Deaths: 9,809

FALLING POPULATION
Rhode Island's 2008 population of just over 1.05 million was down several thousand from the previous year, continuing a trend of yearly population losses. The 2007 count was lower than any year since 2001. Moreover, Rhode Island and Michigan were the only states to lose population in the July 2007 to July 2008 period. Rhode Island is gaining people due to natural increase (births minus deaths), and net international migration (those coming to Rhode Island from abroad minus those leaving). Each of these categories added about 3,000 people to the state population in 2007; however, Rhode Island is hemorrhaging population to other states, losing over 10,000 residents to other US locales during the same period.

MEDIAN AGE
Rhode Island	38.3
US	36.4

Source: Centers for Disease Control and Prevention (CDC).

BIRTH RATE
Rhode Island's birth rate (births per 1,000 population) is 11.6. The rate for the US is 14.2; Utah has the highest rate with 21.0, and Vermont the lowest at 10.4.

Source: CDC.

Did you know. . .

that Rhode Island is the only state which still celebrates Victory Day (otherwise known as V-J Day) commemorating the WWII surrender of Japan to the Allies? The second Monday in August is a legal holiday and local and state government offices are closed, although most businesses remain open.

TAKE 5 ROBIN KALL'S TOP FIVE
RHODE ISLAND READS

Robin Kall is the creator and host of Reading with Robin, a Providence radio talk show which debuted in 2002. The program is heard on WHJJ (AM 920), and is devoted to authors, readers, and their favorite books. Kall is Honorary Chair of the Rhode Island Center for the Book's "Reading Across Rhode Island" program. She is also a leading promoter of the American Cancer Society's "Strides Against Breast Cancer Walk," and the "Walking with Robin" team is a perennial top fundraiser. Robin Kall lives in East Greenwich with her husband, two teenagers and a dog.

1. *Ruby* — **Ann Hood**. A grief stricken thirty-something widow finds a worldly, tough talking, pregnant 15-year-old on the doorstep of her Rhode Island vacation house. West Warwick native Hood lives on Providence's East Side and is the author of a number of books, including *The Knitting Circle: A Novel*.

2. *Confidential Source* — **Jan Brogan**. A page-turning mystery set in lots of familiar Rhode Island locations and featuring corruption, addiction and a lovable protagonist in Hallie Ahern. Former *Providence Journal* reporter Brogan hits all the right spots in this follow up to her debut, *Final Copy!*

3. *R is for Rhode Island Red A Rhode Island Alphabet* — **Mark Allio (writer) and Mary Jane Begin (illustrator)**. A beautifully designed and illustrated children's book that captures Rhode Island's culture, attractions and natural beauty from "A" to "Z." Barrington's Begin has illustrated numerous children's books, collaborating on this title with her husband.

4. *The Memory of Running* — **Ron McLarty**. When an accident kills his parents, an out-of-shape middle-aged loser decides to bicycle from Maine to California. His mission? To claim the remains of his long lost schizophrenic sister, now in a Los Angeles morgue. The quixotic narrator recalls his East Providence childhood during an incident packed journey.

5. *Outside Providence* — **Peter Farrelly**. A coming of age tale that contrasts blue-collar Pawtucket with the tony Connecticut prep school the 16-year-old narrator attends. The 1999 movie adaptation was written by Farrelly and his brother Bobby, and directed by Rhode Islander Michael Corrente.

LIFE EXPECTANCY

Men	75.5	(US 75.4)
Women	80.3	(US 80.7)

Sources: Rhode Island Department of Health, CDC.

POPULATION COMPONENTS

- Percentage of the RI population under 18: 22
- Percentage 65 and over: 14
- Percentage female: 51.7
- Percentage male: 48.3
- Percentage of Rhode Islanders born in the US: 87
- Percentage of Rhode Islanders born within the state: 59
- Percentage 25 years or older who have graduated from high school: 83
- Percentage 25 years or older with a bachelor's degree or higher: 29

Source: US Census Bureau.

ON A TYPICAL DAY IN RHODE ISLAND . . .

- 35 children are born
- 27 people die
- 19 marriages take place
- 8 people divorce

Source: CDC.

Did you know. . .

that Rhode Island drivers are no longer the worst in the US? According to a test administered by GMAC Insurance, Rhode Islanders ranked 41st in the nation in 2008 in driving knowledge. This places the state in the bottom quintile, but is up from Rhode Island's miserable 47th place showing in 2007, and its execrable last place (51 out of 51) performance in 2006.

TAKE 5 TOP FIVE MOST POPULOUS CITIES

1. **Providence**	172,500
2. **Warwick**	85,100
3. **Cranston**	80,500
4. **Pawtucket**	72,300
5. **E. Providence**	48,800

ELEMENTARY AND SECONDARY EDUCATION (2007-08)

- Number of public schools: 338
- Total public school students: 147,629
- Number of school districts: 36
- Number of charter schools: 13
- Number of students enrolled in charter schools: 3,100
- Students attending Catholic schools: 16,000

Did you know...

that Rhode Island has 764 bridges? The state has the regrettable distinction of leading the nation in percentage of "structurally deficient" and "functionally obsolete" bridges.

Did you know...

that the Roger Williams statue located at Roger Williams University in Bristol actually features the face of Ted Williams, the famed Boston Red Sox slugger of the 1940s and 1950s? There were no definitive images of Roger Williams created in his lifetime, and so North Scituate sculptor Armand LaMontagne used the visage of "the Splendid Splinter" in his stead. The Pawtucket-born LaMontagne also created the Ted Williams statue for the Baseball Hall of Fame.

- Students attending independent non-Catholic schools: 12,208
- Per pupil spending: $11,769
- Per pupil spending rank in the US: 6th

Sources: Rhode Island Department of Elementary and Secondary Education, National Center for Education Statistics, US Census Bureau, Providence Journal.

Brown University

Brown University, founded in 1764 as "The College of Rhode Island" in Warren, moved to the East Side of Providence in 1770. Originally a Baptist institution, it acquired the Brown name in 1804 in honor of benefactor Nicholas Brown, a leading Providence businessman of the time. Brown is one of eight Ivy League schools, and is the seventh oldest college in the nation.

Brown admitted its first woman in 1891 with the establishment of a parallel Women's College, which received the name Pembroke College in 1928 and merged entirely with Brown in 1971. Brown is well-known for an innovative undergraduate curriculum which allows students unusual latitude in choosing their course of study. This "New Curriculum" evolved in 1969-70 and was conceived by students.

Brown's long history has lately seemed as much of a liability as an asset. Brown's current president is Ruth J. Simmons who became the first African American to head an Ivy League institution when she assumed the position in 2001. In 2003, Simmons appointed a committee to study Brown's relationship to the slave trade. The committee's "Slavery and Justice" report was released in 2006 and noted that the Brown family were slave owners and traders, and that the college's first president, Reverend James Manning, was also a slave owner. Moreover, slave labor was used in the construction of Brown's oldest building, University Hall, and the slave trade was used to generate Brown's endowment. The report recommended social justice efforts, memorials and educational measures that would acknowledge the college's historic ties to slavery, and attempt to make some redress.

HIGHER EDUCATION

Rhode Island is home to over a dozen postsecondary institutions enrolling more than 80,000 students. Brown University is the best known, but the Rhode Island School of Design (RISD) and the US Naval War College (NWC) in Newport aren't far behind. RISD has spawned a number of big shot artists, while the NWC has its own War Gaming Department.

The University of Rhode Island (URI) is the state's largest university and was established in 1892 as an agricultural school. URI is locat-

TAKE 5 TOP FIVE THINGS NAMED AFTER ROGER WILLIAMS, RHODE ISLAND'S FOUNDER

1. **Roger Williams Park**, Providence. The 430-acre Victorian era park includes a zoo, natural history museum, carousel, botanical center and other attractions.

2. **Roger Williams University**, Bristol. The university occupies 140 acres on Mount Hope Bay in Bristol. Originally chartered as Roger Williams Junior College in 1956, it moved from Providence to its current location in 1969. Younger students can attend Roger Williams Middle School in south Providence.

3. **Roger Williams Medical Center (RWMC)**, Providence. Located in the Mount Pleasant neighborhood of Providence, RWMC specializes in geriatric care and cancer related services.

4. **Roger Williams National Memorial**, Providence. The memorial comprises a small area just north of downtown Providence near where Williams and the other colonists lived. The park-like memorial is run by the National Park Service and has a visitors' center staffed by a ranger.

5. **Roger Williams Inn**, home of the Westerly International Hostel, Westerly. Located in downtown Westerly and constructed in 1880, the inn offers private and shared accommodation for travelers on a budget.

They said it

"A smudge in the fast lane on the way to Cape Cod."
**– Journalist Steve Morin describing Rhode Island
in the *Wall Street Journal* in 1983.**

ed in Kingston, and is renowned for its Graduate School of Oceanography. Rhode Island College (RIC) is in Providence, and was founded in the 1850s as a teacher's college. The Community College of Rhode Island (CCRI) has four campuses throughout the state.

Johnson and Wales University, the state's largest private university, has one of the top culinary arts programs in the country, and New England Tech in Warwick is known for automotive and computer technology. Other Rhode Island colleges include Smithfield's Bryant University, which boasts a top-flight business school, and Roger Williams University in Bristol, home to Rhode Island's only law school. Salve Regina University, a Catholic institution founded by the Sisters of Mercy, occupies a number of the famed Newport Mansions overlooking Rhode Island Sound. Providence College (PC) is also a Catholic school; it was founded by the Diocese of Providence and the Dominican Friars, and has a strong undergraduate liberal arts program, not to mention a top-flight basketball team.

They said it

"[Rhode Island] is a place where politics and governance have been an everchanging soap opera and spectator sport. It is a place of natural beauty and resources unduplicated anywhere in the country, providing a quality of life that natives and wannabes are fiercely proud of."
**– *Rhode Island Monthly* President and Publisher John J. Palumbo in
the twentieth anniversary edition of the magazine in May 2008.**

They said it

"Beginning as an unpromising collection of outcasts, malcontents, squatters, and dissenters, followed by a century and a half of internal dissension and external hostility, Rhode Island emerged as a special place."

– Historians George H. Kellner and J. Stanley Lemons,
Rhode Island The Independent State.

College	Founding	Main Campus	Total Students
Brown University	1764	Providence (East Side)	8,200
RI College	1854	Providence (Mt. Pleasant)	9,000
Bryant University	1863	Smithfield	3,600
RI School of Design	1877	Providence (East Side)	2,200
US Naval War College	1884	Newport	600
University of RI	1892	Kingston	16,000
Johnson & Wales University	1914	Providence (Downtown)	10,000
Providence College	1917	Providence (Elmhurst)	5,300
Salve Regina U	1934	Newport	2,500
New England Tech	1940	Warwick	3,000
Roger Williams U	1956	Bristol	5,100
Community College of RI	1964	Warwick, Lincoln, Providence, Newport	16,000

Did you know...

that more than 72 percent of all Rhode Island newborns are delivered at Providence's Women & Infants Hospital? Women and Infants' 9,462 deliveries in 2007 ranked seventh in the nation.

MAJOR RHODE ISLAND HOSPITALS

Hospital Name	Location	Founding	Beds
Butler	Providence	1844	117
Rhode Island	Providence	1863	719
Newport	Newport	1873	129
Landmark Med Ctr	Woonsocket	1873	214
Roger Williams Med Ctr	Providence	1878	146
Women & Infants'	Providence	1884	197
Our Lady of Fatima	N. Providence	1892	269
Miriam	Providence	1902	247
Memorial	Pawtucket	1910	294
South County	Wakefield	1919	100
Westerly	Westerly	1925	125
VA Medical Ctr	Providence	1949	119
Kent	Warwick	1951	359

COMMUNICATIONS

NEWSPAPERS AND MAGAZINES: *The Providence Journal* is available statewide and has a circulation of 149,000, ranking 73rd among US dailies. The state's other dailies are Woonsocket's *The Call*, *The Kent County Daily Times*, *The Warwick Daily Times*, Pawtucket's *The Times*, the *Newport Daily News* and the *Westerly Sun*. In addition to the dailies, there are dozens of other papers, many of them small town weeklies, as well as student, ethnic, foreign language, religious and niche publications. Among the more prominent weeklies is the *Providence Phoenix*, a free alternative paper with a circulation of 60,000, which covers Rhode Island politics, arts and entertainment. The best known monthly is the glossy *Rhode Island Monthly* whose "Best of Rhode Island" edition is among several special issues it publishes yearly.

Slang

Rhode Island, or Roe Dye-lin' as it is known locally, is a magical linguistic world filled with bubblers that are side by each, and kids who, not fuh nothin', look like theyuh gonna end up at the ACI, but then go on to graduate Rick and stah on stage at Pee-pack. The Rhody accent has been described as a cross between those of Boston and Brooklyn, which is like mating two very ugly breeds of dog. Collahs to talk radio invariably get hot under the collah about the guv-uh-nuh or may-uh's latest idear to rescue the state from financial rune.

Rhode Island's distinctive accent and slang is such a rich topic that one could write a whole book on it, and in fact *Providence Journal* writer Mark Patinkin, along with illustrator Don Bousquet, did just that in 1993 with *The Rhode Island Dictionary*. The book, which codified such classics as "jeet?" for "did you eat?" and "P.S.D.S." for "pierced ears" is still in print, a testimony to the affection Roe Dye-linders have for their lingo.

The following is a micro-list of Rhode Island terminology; for language related to Rhode Island cuisine, see the "Food and Drink" chapter.

ACI: Adult Correctional Institute — the prisons in Cranston.

Bubbler: Water fountain, pronounced "bubluh."

Carvone: A pompous, obnoxious, disgusting, uncultured person. Often used by Italian-Americans.

CF: City of Central Falls.

Chariho: A school district serving the southern Rhode Island towns of Charlestown, Richmond and Hopkinton.

CCRI: Community College of Rhode Island. Also known as CC or "See-See," and formerly called Rhode Island Junior College or RIJC, pronounced phonetically as "reject" by some.

Cumbies: Cumberland Farms (Cum-buh-lan Fahms) convenience store.

Down cellar (celluh): Basement. A New England usage.

TAKE 5 CRYSTAL SARGENT'S TOP FIVE
WAYS TO DETECT A RHODE ISLAND ACCENT

Crystal Sargent and Jacqueline Gorman are Middletown speech pathologists. They operate "Accent Your Options," part of a speech and language therapy practice. Most of their accent clients are non-native English speakers seeking to advance professionally, but some are natives hoping to refine their Rhody pronunciation.

1. **Reduction of the "r":** "Work" becomes "wuhk," and "lobster" becomes "lobstah."
2. **Addition of an "r":** "Pasta" becomes "pastur," and "idea" becomes "idear."
3. **Elongation of vowels:** "Cranston" becomes "Creeeanston," and "that" becomes "theeat."
4. **Syllable reduction:** "Saturday" becomes "Satdee."
5. **Glottal stop:** "Lit-tle" becomes "li-uh," and "but-ton" becomes "but-un."

TAKE 5 FIVE RHODE ISLAND HOMONYMS

1. **Party and Potty**. Chil'ren should yuze tha' potty befawa the pahty, soze they don' have a accidin'.

2. **Dark and Dock**. I doan think it's real smott to be playin' on the dock aftah dahk like ure doin'; they might even be shocks in that watah, ya nevah know.

3. **Wood and Word.** Mock my woulds, he ain' gonna find no deer in them woods, 'specially after the numbuh a beeahs he's had.

4. **Anchor and Anka** (as in Paul). What a on-uh it was to meet Paul Anker aftuh his show at the Tent. I even got him to sign a little souveneeah an-kuh chahm I braht wit me.

5. **Morse and Moss**. Can you believe it? He knows mawhs code, nobody luhns that no more. It's cuz he was in the Navy all doze yeeahs.

Downcity: Downtown Providence; the term was out of use for some time, but was reintroduced in the 1990s in an effort to rebrand the city as an arts and entertainment destination.

The Dunk: The Dunkin' Donuts Center. The sports arena and entertainment venue in downtown Providence was formerly known as the "Civic Centuh."

East Bay: Towns on the east side of Narragansett Bay including Warren, Barrington and Bristol.

The Hill: Federal Hill, the traditionally Italian American neighborhood just west of downtown Providence.

I'm all set: "I'm fine," or "I don't need anything further." Not unique to Rhode Island, but very prevalent. Rhody bank teller as she hands over bag of money to robber: "Ya need to get in the safe?"
Robber: "Nah, I'm all set."

TAKE 5 CHARLIE HALL'S TOP FIVE MOST LAMPOONABLE RHODE ISLANDERS

Comedian, writer and performer Charlie Hall is the creative force behind the Ocean State Follies, the cabaret that has poked fun at the "state" of Rhode Island since 1991. *Rhode Island Monthly* magazine has included the Follies and Charlie Hall on their "Best of Rhode Island" lists numerous times. Hall is also behind the Rhode Island Comedy Festival and other productions, and his cartoons have been included in several editions of the Best Editorial Cartoons of the Year. Hall has written and published three books, including *Hot Sketch: The Cartoons of Rhode Island Funnyman Charlie Hall*, and *Hot Sketch 2: The Independent Funnyman*. In addition to live performances, you can find Charlie and the Follies at www.oceanstatefollies.com.

1. **Buddy Cianci**. The Motherlode of local political parody. Mayor, then felon, then mayor, then felon again. Quick-witted, smart, charming, narcissistic, control-freak; doesn't get mad - gets even.

2. **Bruce Sundlun**. Former governor (or King of Sund-land, he'd prefer). Shoots off his mouth as often as he shoots raccoons. Gets late night urges for plastic forks. Great sense of humor, ornery, opinionated, and a true gentleman. Wants to run for mayor of Garden City.

3. **Arlene Violet**. Ex-nun, ex-attorney general, ex-radio talk show host. Can't hold a job evidently. Passionate and fearless, calls 'em as she sees 'em. Well worthy of her "Attila the Nun" nickname. Heavy Rhody accent: Last pronounced an "r" in 1968.

4. **Richard Hatch**. From Middletown, the first winner on the reality show *Survivor*, somehow "forgot" to pay taxes on the one million dollar prize he accepted in front of 30 million viewers live on TV. Called the "fat, naked guy" by David Letterman, filling all of RI with pride.

5. **The Cardi Brothers (aka Nirope)**. The perfect threesome—but not in the good way. As generous as the day is long, but their TV and radio commercials play every three minutes, of every hour, of every day, on every TV and radio station in southern New England. **Honorable mentions:** Salty Brine, Doug White, Gene Valicenti, Roanne from Off-Track Bedding, Karen Adams, Don Carcieri and David Cicilline.

TAKE 5 FIVE TIPS FOR TALKING LOCAL
ABOUT LOCALITIES

1. **Pawtucket**. The "w" is silent; it's Puh-TUCK-et, not PAW-tuck-et.
2. **Warwick**. Some Rhode Islanders omit the second "w," saying "War-ick," others snatch the "r" and say "Waw-ick."
3. **Woonsocket**. Don't pronounce the double "o"; it's "One-socket."
4. **Coventry**. Universally pronounced as "CAH-ven-TREE.
5. **Burrillville**. Typically pronounced "Burra-ville."

Italian sports page: The obituaries.

Not for nothing: A choice nugget or opinion, the inside dope which you can take for what it's worth. *Not fuh nothin', but just between you and me, and I'm not sayin' it's so, but what's goin' on down they-uh is way out of hand, at least from what I'm hearin' anyway.*

PawSox: Pawtucket Red Sox baseball team, the AAA affiliate of the Boston Red Sox.

PPAC: Providence Performing Arts Center, pronounced Pee-Pack.

Red Bridge: The bridge linking Providence's East Side to East Providence. Its official name is the Henderson Bridge and it opened in 1969; the name comes from its precursor, the long since demolished Red Bridge.

Rhode Island roll: Tapping the breaks ever so slightly at stop signs, rather than coming to a complete halt.

RIC: Rhode Island College, pronounced "Rick."

Side by each: Side by side. A Woonsocketism popular with people of French Canadian descent.

TAKE 5 FIVE UNUSUAL RHODE ISLAND SPORTING PURSUITS

1. **Providence Roller Derby**. Billed as "New England's first all women's flat-track roller derby league," Providence Roller Derby was founded in 2004 by a Brown University alumna. Teams include the Sakonnet River Roller Rats and the Rhode Island Riveters.

2. **Providence Grays Vintage Baseball Club**. Some people recreate Civil War battles, these guys channel the 1884 Providence Grays baseball team using the rules, uniforms and equipment (or lack thereof) of that era. Batters can request high or low pitches, and it takes six balls to draw a walk. Games against like-minded teams including the Rhode Island Game Hens and Bristol Blues are played at locations around the state.

3. **Newport International Polo Series**. Newport was at one time the world's international polo capital, but WWI and the Depression ended that happy time in the sun. The Newport Polo Club inaugurated the International Polo Series in 1992; it features domestic battles as well as visiting squads from England, Ireland, France, Egypt, South Africa and elsewhere. Matches are held at 100-acre Glen Farm in Portsmouth, a property which dates to the 1600s.

4. **Newport Grand Jai Alai** (closed in 2003). The fastest game in the world was played at the Newport Grand fronton from 1976 until 2003. A highly entertaining gambling vehicle played primarily by Spanish Basques, jai alai is rare in the US outside Florida. It was popular with local bettors before slots became widespread and the Connecticut casinos opened.

5. **Ocean State Curling Club**. The North Smithfield based Ocean State Curling Club is the place to bone up on a Scottish sport that some call "chess on ice." Popular in Canada, curling involves the strategic sliding of 40-pound granite rocks across a sheet of ice.

Smith Street/Smith Hill: Used to indicate the Rhode Island General Assembly's location.

South County: Rhode Island mainland's southern section, technically Washington County.

Swamp Yankee: A rural Rhode Islander, particularly someone who could be described as stubborn, old fashioned, and thrifty.

Training School: The juvenile detention facility in Cranston.

Triple-Decker: A three-story three-unit dwelling with front balconies common in the older industrialized cities of Providence, Pawtucket and Woonsocket. The triple-decker structure allows for three generations to live under one roof, although not in the same unit.

V-J Day: Victory over Japan Day commemorating the end of World War II. The holiday is celebrated on the second Monday in August, and is unique to Rhode Island.

West Bay: Areas on the west side of Narragansett Bay including Cranston, Warwick and East Greenwich.

Wicked: An enduring southern New England intensifier. Traffic on the 95 can be "wicked slow" at rush hour.

Cities and Towns

The names of Rhode Island's cities and towns are typically inspired by English locales (Bristol, Coventry), a notable person (Lincoln, Foster), or an aspect of the landscape, either in English (Central Falls) or a Native language (Woonsocket). The names can be confusing, as many cities and towns are amalgamations of several villages. For example, a person may rightfully claim to be from Pascoag or Wakefield, but these are pieces of the larger municipalities of Burrillville and South Kingstown respectively.

Barrington (16,444): The name is believed to be derived from Barrington Parish in Somerset, England, home of many of Barrington's first settlers. Barrington separated from Swansea, MA in 1717 and joined RI in 1746. After some years as a part of Warren, it was incorporated under its current name in 1770. Barrington is home to the Rhode Island Country Club, a top flight golf course on Narragansett Bay.

Bristol (22,552): Founded in 1680 and named after the eponymous English city, Bristol was originally part of Plymouth County, MA. Famous for hosting the oldest continuing Fourth of July celebration in the nation, Bristol is also home to Roger Williams University, Colt State Park, the Hershehoff Marine Museum and America's Cup Hall of Fame, Blithewold Mansion, Gardens & Arboretum, and Linden Place.

Burrillville (16,563): Inhabited since the late 1600s and incorporated in 1806, Burrillville is located in the rural northwest corner of the state and is composed of ten villages. Prior to incorporation, it was part of Glocester.

Central Falls (18,823): Central Falls is a mere 1.3 square miles and is surrounded by Cumberland, Lincoln and Pawtucket. It is one of the smallest and meatiest cities in the US with a density of about 15,000 people per square mile. Central Falls was a booming textile town in the 1800s, and at one time was also home to a chocolate factory, earning it the sobriquet "chocolatemills" or "chocolateville." It takes its name from falls in the Blackstone River, and was incorporated in 1895. Prior to becoming its own municipality, Central Falls was a part of Smithfield, and later, Lincoln.

Charlestown (8,120): A popular southern Rhode Island beach spot, and prior to the arrival of the Europeans, a long-standing Narragansett Indian settlement, Charlestown was founded in 1738 when a portion of Westerly was separated and incorporated. Charlestown is home to Ninigret Park, Burlingame State Park and nearly 2,000 acres of Narragansett tribal land.

Coventry (34,510): Coventry was established in 1639 and incorporated in 1743 after having been purchased and set off from Warwick. The town is named after Coventry, England. It is residential in its eastern sections, and rural in its western areas bordering Connecticut.

Cranston (80,463): Cranston is Rhode Island's third largest city after Providence and Warwick. The area's settlement dates to 1638 when Roger Williams purchased land for settlement in the Pawtuxet area where the Pawtuxet River flows into upper Narragansett Bay. Cranston was incorporated as a town in 1754 and became a city in 1910. Over the years, it ceded territory to its northern neighbor, Providence, including the site of Roger

Williams Park. The city was named after Samuel Cranston, Governor of Rhode Island from 1698 to 1727. Cranston has a long agricultural and industrial history, and is a mix of high-density residential in its eastern section, and suburban and rural areas in its western area.

Cumberland (34,314): Cumberland was the first European-settled site in Rhode Island. William Blackstone built a home in the Londsdale area in 1635, preceding Rhode Island founder Roger Williams by a year. The town takes its name from Cumberland, England and was originally part of the Massachusetts town of Rehoboth which comprised a number of towns and villages in present day northeastern Rhode Island and southeastern Massachusetts. Cumberland, previously known as Attleborough Gore, was obtained from Massachusetts and incorporated in 1746.

East Greenwich (13,349): East Greenwich was acquired by King Charles II from the Pequot Indians in 1644, and incorporated in 1677. Until 1854, its 1804-built Town Hall served as one of Rhode Island's five original state houses. East Greenwich is on Narragansett Bay, and is named after Greenwich County in Kent, England.

East Providence (48,779): The "Gateway to the East Bay" was settled in 1636 by Roger Williams and his associates. For a long time it was part of the Massachusetts town of Seekonk, but was incorporated in 1862 as the Rhode Island town of East Providence. It is home to the Loof Carousel, a National Historic Landmark which has also been designated the State Symbol of American Folk Art.

Exeter (6,195): Exeter is named after the English town and is home to the Arcadia Wildlife Management Area as well as Yawgoo Valley, Rhode Island's only ski area. The town was formed in 1742 when North Kingstown's western area was partitioned.

Foster (4,511): Rural Foster is in the forested western part of the state. It was incorporated in 1781 when it separated from Scituate. Foster's origins date to 1662 when a large piece of land called West Quanaug was purchased by colonists from local Indians. The name comes from Theodore Foster, who advocated for Rhode Island joining the Union and was a US Senator from 1790 to 1803.

TAKE 5 LINCOLN CHAFEE'S FIVE POINTS ON A RHODE ISLAND TREASURE HUNT

Lincoln Chafee is a distinguished visiting fellow at Brown University's Watson Institute for International Studies. A native Rhode Islander, Chafee received a classics degree from Brown in 1975, and then spent seven years as a blacksmith shoeing horses at racetracks in the US and western Canada. Once back in Rhode Island, Mr. Chafee served on the Warwick City Council and then as Warwick mayor for four terms. Upon the 1999 death of his father, Senator John Chafee, Lincoln Chafee was appointed to his place in the US Senate, completing the final year of the elder Chafee's term. In 2000, Lincoln Chafee was elected to the US Senate as a Republican, and served on several key Senate committees. Chafee was defeated in a 2006 reelection bid, and subsequently left the Republican Party, with which he had become increasingly disenchanted. Lincoln Chafee is author of the 2008 book *Against the Tide: How a Compliant Congress Empowered a Reckless President*.

1. **Jerimoth Hill**. Rhode Island's highest point, Foster.
2. **Tomaquag Indian Memorial Museum**. Exeter.
3. **Weekapaug Breachway**. Westerly; lies two miles from Misquamicut State Beach and connects Block Island Sound to Winnapaug Pond.
4. **Little Compton Common**. One of Rhode Island's rare village greens.
5. **The 1663 King Charles II Charter**. Guarantees Rhode Islanders religious freedom and the right to govern themselves. Displayed on the second floor of the State House.

Glocester (10,536): Glocester, a rural community in northwestern Rhode Island, was established in 1639 and formed part of the land Roger Williams received from local Indian tribes. The town separated from Providence in 1731 and takes its name from Frederick Lewis, Duke of Gloucester, who was King George II's son. The Glocester village of Chepachet hosts the annual Ancients and Horribles parade.

Hopkinton (8,003): Located in the state's southwest corner on the Pawcatuck River on the Connecticut border, Hopkinton is composed of the villages of Ashaway, Bradford, Hope Valley and Rockville. Hopkinton was founded as part of Westerly in 1669, and was incorporated as its own town in 1757. It was named after Stephen Hopkins, a Rhode Island Governor and signer of the Declaration of Independence.

Jamestown (5,515): Jamestown is on Conanicut Island (named after Sachem Canonicus) in Narragansett Bay. It is linked to the western mainland of Rhode Island by the Jamestown Verrazzano Bridge and to Aquidneck Island by the Newport Pell Bridge. Prior to the construction of the Jamestown Bridge, access to Conanicut Island was by ferry only. One of the earliest European settlements in Rhode Island, Conanicut Island was purchased by Newport settlers in 1656; Jamestown was incorporated in 1678 and named after Prince James, later James II.

Johnston (28,680): Johnston was settled in 1680 and incorporated in 1759 when it split from Providence. Its name is derived from Augustus Lucas Johnston, who served as Rhode Island Attorney General from 1758 to 1766 and was a major area landowner. Primarily a Providence suburb, Johnston is also home to a number of farms, as well as the state landfill, otherwise known as the Rhode Island Resource Recovery Corporation.

Providence

Providence is the state capital and Rhode Island's largest city. With over 172,000 people, it is the third most populous city in New England, just slightly behind Worcester, MA. Providence is also the anchor of a 1.6 million person metropolitan statistical area that takes in much of Rhode Island and southeastern Massachusetts.

Founded in 1636 by Massachusetts Bay Colony exile Roger Williams, Providence is so named to honor God's "Providence" in providing refuge to the persecuted. Providence would become a leading industrial and financial center, but for its first several decades was a sleepy farming and fishing village. It was nearly obliterated in 1676 during King Philip's War, but gradually rebuilt and by the 1760s was a thriving town with a range of shops, tradesmen and mercantile activities. Providence played an important role in the American Revolution, including the burning of the British ship *The Gaspee* in nearby Pawtuxet Cove in 1772, and tea burning in Market Square in 1775.

In the post-Revolutionary period, Providence displaced Newport as the area's major port, and became one of the new nation's leading commercial centers. In the 1800s, Providence and surrounding towns became leaders in the production of textiles, as well as jewelry, silverware, metals, machinery, tools and rubber goods. Throughout the 1800s, Providence grew and modernized as railroads allowed for the efficient transport of manufactured goods, and a horse-powered street car system (later electrified) debuted on city streets. The city also became a magnet for immigrants from Ireland, Britain, northern Europe, Quebec, and Italy, most of whom who lived in distinct ethnic enclaves. By the turn of the twentieth century, Providence was a prosperous city with plenty of showy mansions and impressive public buildings, including its 1878 Second Empire inspired City Hall. Downtown Providence of the 1920s was a whirl of theatres, department stores and office buildings, and the city's 1930 population exceeded 250,000. Providence then went into decline, losing nearly 40 percent of its population between 1940 and 1980, before rebounding in the 1990s. The current population is approximately what it was in 1900.

Providence's industrial base suffered mightily during the Depression, and in the post WWII period the city also lost significant amounts of its retail activity to outlying areas. Moreover, the construction of the I-95 and I-195 freeways scarred the city's landscape, and spurred suburban development at the capital city's expense. Providence became increasingly poor and run-down, and was saddled with the "armpit of New England" tag.

Since the 1970s, Providence has reinvented itself. No longer a manufacturing hub or even a major retailing center, Providence's strengths include government, medical and educational institutions, non-profits, and the city's status as an arts and entertainment destination. Brown University, RISD, Providence College, Rhode Island College and Johnson & Wales University are all within Providence's borders, as are several major hospitals. The city is renowned for its architecture, which is not limited to Benefit Street and College Hill, but also includes marquee buildings downtown as well as in several neighborhoods. Providence's cultural institutions include Trinity Repertory Company, the Providence Performing Arts Center and the RISD Museum. The downtown Convention Center and Dunkin' Donuts Arena are regional draws.

The finishing touches on Providence's rebirth came in the 1990s: Train tracks were moved and the Providence River uncovered and altered to allow the creation of Waterplace Park, the scene of WaterFire. The Providence Place Mall opened in 1999, reintroducing department stores to downtown, while the Federal Hill neighborhood reasserted itself and began drawing larger and better heeled crowds.

Renaissances aside, and despite its top rated colleges, great restaurants, and cultural amenities, Providence is still a poor city. Outside of the mostly affluent East Side and a few other pockets, the city has a high poverty rate and low performing schools. When the housing bubble popped, many of Providence's poorer neighborhoods became dotted with foreclosure signs and abandoned buildings, depressing property values and city revenues. Still, Providence retains a unique character and history, and in the face of the homogenization that has beset so many US cities, remains a beacon of individuality and creativity.

Lincoln (22,105): Lincoln, named after the president, was incorporated in 1871 when it separated from Smithfield. In 1895, part of Lincoln's territory was ceded to form the city of Central Falls. European settlement in the area dates to the mid-1600s, and Lincoln is home to the 1693 Eleazer Arnold House, one of the oldest residences in Rhode Island. Other attractions include the 627-acre Lincoln Woods State Park and Twin River Casino's 4,700 slot machines.

Little Compton (3,535): Little Compton is bounded by the Sakonnet River in Narragansett Bay and the state of Massachusetts. It retains an agricultural character and is also a popular tourist destination. It was established in 1682 and incorporated in 1746 when it was transferred from the Plymouth Colony to Rhode Island. Little Compton was home to the Sakonnet Indians, and spawned the Rhode Island Red chicken, the state bird.

Middletown (16,259): Middletown is located on Aquidneck Island between Newport and Portsmouth, and is named for this central location. Middletown was incorporated in 1731 when it was set off from Newport. During that city's colonial heyday, Middletown was a popular country get-away spot for well-to-do Newporters.

Narragansett (16,511): Narragansett was incorporated in 1901 when it separated from South Kingstown, although European settlement in the area dates to 1675. Narragansett has long been a tourist favorite and has some of southern New England's most famous beaches. It's also home to the Point Judith Lighthouse and the Galilee fishing port. Narragansett was hard hit by a fire in 1900, as well as the 1938 hurricane.

New Shoreham (1,021): New Shoreham is Block Island's sole municipality. Block Island is at the mouth of Long Island Sound, and was named after Dutch explorer Adrian Block who visited it in 1614. It was settled in 1661 and became part of Rhode Island in 1664. Block Island's population swells to 10,000 in the summer when vacationers descend upon it. The Island's current reputation for carefree good times belies its early history of shipwrecks and piracy.

North Kingstown (26,708): North Kingstown's origins date to 1637 when Roger Williams established a trading post at the intersection of two Native American thoroughfares. Williams lived in the area between 1643 and 1651. Kings Towne was incorporated in 1674, and divided into North and South in 1722. North Kingstown is the birthplace of the US Navy Seabees, and is home to the Quonset Port and Commerce Park at Davisville. The Gilbert Stuart Birthplace and Museum is located in the village of Saunderstown.

North Providence (32,885): North Providence was settled in 1636 and incorporated as a town in 1765 when it separated from Providence. However, by 1875 North Providence was a fraction of its former size as it lost territory to Providence and Pawtucket. The city today is primarily suburban.

North Smithfield (11,294): North Smithfield was incorporated in 1871 when it was set off from Smithfield. North Smithfield is anchored by Slatersville, which was established in 1807 as the first planned industrial village in the country.

Pawtucket (72,342): The name comes from a Native American word for "falls." Pawtucket is the fourth largest municipality in the state and was incorporated in 1828 when it was still part of Massachusetts. It was transferred to Rhode Island in 1862, expanded in 1874 and incorporated with the city designation in 1885. First settled in 1655, Pawtucket became famous in the 1790s when mills were established on the Blackstone River, heralding the start of the American Industrial Revolution. Pawtucket is home to the nearly 200-acre Slater Memorial Park, the Slater Mill Historic Site, McCoy Stadium (home of the Pawtucket Red Sox AAA baseball team) and an arts district oriented around former mills on the Blackstone River.

TAKE 5 DAVID BRUSSAT'S FIVE BEST
(AND FIVE WORST) PROVIDENCE BUILDINGS

David Brussat is a member of the *Providence Journal's* Editorial Board and writes weekly on architecture and urbanism in Rhode Island and elsewhere. He is particularly interested in downtown Providence, and sometimes pens his *Journal* column under the "Dr. Downtown" moniker.

FIVE BEST

1. **State House**. 1901. Beaux Arts masterpiece by the nation's premier architects, McKim, Mead & White. Unfortunately, a beautiful work environment hasn't cleansed the state's politics.

2. **The Arcade**. 1828. Between Westminster and Weybosset streets. Nation's oldest (not first) indoor shopping mall. Competing Greek Revival facades by James C. Bucklin and Russell Warren. Its granite columns, six per facade, were the nation's largest monoliths. Arcade opened to jeers from Providence's existing commercial district, Cheapside, on North Main, but commerce jumped the river, proving "Butler's Folly" (after developer Cyrus Butler) no joke.

3. **Industrial Trust Building**. 1928. Kennedy Plaza. Tallest building in state. Upthrusting masterpiece of Art Deco design atop site of Butler Exchange (headquarters of tycoon Cyrus Butler, of Arcade fame). Often called "the Superman Building," although the television version of the comic book skyscraper was actually modeled on Los Angeles City Hall. Zeppelin gondola on east facade and interior decor anticipated building's role, unfulfilled, as airship station.

4. **Providence County Superior Courthouse**. 1933. 250 Benefit Street. Home also of Rhode Island Supreme Court, and one of the world's largest Georgian Revival buildings. Adored by H.P. Lovecraft. Design features succession of gabled brick masses gracefully climbing College Hill in two parallel wings, linked by colonnade on South Main.

5. **Providence Place**. 1999. Traditional design by Friedrich St. Florian delights the eye, even if some of its detail is lame. Highlighted return of traditional architecture to Providence. Helped bring life back downtown. Its huge financial success rebutted opposition to downtown mall led by suburban mall interests.

Outside Providence honorable mention: Redwood Library and Athenaeum (Newport).

FIVE WORST

1. **GTECH World Headquarters**. 2006. Memorial Boulevard, opposite Providence Place. "Ice Cube in Diapers." Gray glass box atop garage. Halted revival of traditional design in Capital Center, downtown's new district; aborted urban-planning success. Capital Center Commission sought architectural novelty, got predictable hodgepodge instead. Shame! Best that can be said of it: Reflects superior architecture in windows.

2. **Old Stone Square**. 1984. 31 South Main Street. "Rubik's Cube." Glass and granite box minus its upper northwestern quadrant. Designed by celebrated modernist Edward Larrabee Barnes after struggle to preserve beauty of College Hill, and widely supposed as intended to irk local preservationists. Best that can be said of it: Striking design, should be somewhere else.

3. **Chace Center, RISD Museum of Art**. 2008. 20 North Main Street. "[Insert derisive moniker here]" Glass box atop brick platform. By celebrity architect Jose Rafael Moneo. Continues campaign to ruin beauty of College Hill. Doesn't fit into North Main Street. High cost exposed warped college priorities. Best that can be said of it: Budget cuts stunted height.

4. **Broadcast House**. 1979. 111 Dorrance Street. "East German Embassy." Originally TV station owned by Outlet Communications; now library of Johnson & Wales University. Outlet chief (later governor) Bruce Sundlun allegedly switched from brick to black granite after visiting CBS headquarters at Rockefeller Center. Best that can be said of it . . .

5. **Howard Building**. 1959. Westminster & Dorrance Streets. Three prior Howards on site; first two by Thomas Tefft, third by James Bucklin. Damage by Hurricane Carol (1954) led to fourth. Concrete design by Albert Harkness and Peter Geddes, tarted up with classical "accents" in pink Dryvit in 1987, again in 2003. Best that can be said of it: Bring on Howard V!

Outside Providence dishonorable mention: Community College of Rhode Island's Warwick campus

Portsmouth (17,030): Billed as the "Birthplace of American Democracy," Portsmouth was settled in 1638 by Anne Hutchinson, making it the first community in the Americas established by a woman. Portsmouth occupies the northern part of Aquidneck Island, and takes its name from the English town of the same name. It was the scene of the 1778 "Battle of Rhode Island" in which the Americans with the aid of the French tried to reclaim Aquidneck Island from the British. Portsmouth is home to the Green Animals Topiary Garden and Prudence Island's Sandy Point Lighthouse.

Newport

Newport has worn many hats during its illustrious history: bucolic sheep farming outpost, prosperous port, extravagant home away from home for Gilded Age industrial barons, and, since WWII, popular tourist and cultural spot renowned for its music festivals, restaurants and historical sites.

Newport is located on the southern tip of Aquidneck Island. It was founded in 1639 when a group of settlers moved south from newly established Portsmouth. Newport, like Providence, was founded on the basis of religious toleration, and early on was home to two much persecuted groups: the Quakers and the Jews. In its early days, Newport was a prosperous agricultural settlement and the town's 1696 official seal featured a sheep, not a ship. By the late 1600s Newport, along with Boston, Philadelphia, Charleston and New Amsterdam (New York) was one of America's five largest cities.

In the 1700s, maritime trade supplanted agriculture. Shipbuilding became an important industry, and associated crafts and merchants mushroomed. Newport traded with other major ports on the eastern US seaboard, as well as Europe and the Caribbean. Newport's thriving cultural life and elegant buildings, embodied in the 1748 Redwood Library and Athenaeum, belied the fact that the city was a key center in the American slave trade, a major producer of rum and the scene of piracy.

Newport's dominance as a commercial center would fade toward the end of the eighteenth century. The Revolutionary War period,

Richmond (7,659): Richmond was set off from Charlestown in 1747 and named in honor of William Richmond, a military man and Rhode Island patriot during the Revolutionary era. Richmond is host to the annual Washington County Fair.

Scituate (10,870): Scituate got its name from Scituate, MA from whence a group of settlers came in 1710. The name is derived from the Native word "satuit" meaning "cold brook." Scituate separated from Providence and was incorporated in 1731. The town is the home of the Scituate Reservoir, supplier of metro Providence's drinking water.

during which Newport was occupied by the British and lost half its population, was the beginning of the city's decline relative to other areas. The shipping industry collapsed, and Newport did not develop substantial manufacturing industries as was the case in northern Rhode Island. The Great Gale of 1815 further devastated the city, and in the decades thereafter, Newport became the place where the Northeast's monied elite plied their yachts and swang their croquet mallets, rather than where they made their fortunes.

The late 1800s and early 1900s were Newport's golden age as a high-end resort, but varied factors including the introduction of the income tax, the Depression, and the advent of the jet age and World War II changed the landscape of the country and of the super rich. A diminished Newport Society scene would linger on, but no longer would 70-room houses be commissioned.

Since World War II, Newport has retained its place as a tourist mecca by emphasizing its past and opening itself up to the middle class. Most present day visitors don't arrive with a retinue of servants, but are content to spend a week, weekend or just a day walking the city's cobbled streets, taking in a show at the Newport Jazz or Folk Festival or unwinding in a pub or restaurant. Newport's spectacular coastal setting and large and well-preserved collection of historic buildings guarantee that will it never go out of style as a destination for visitors.

Smithfield (21,279): Smithfield was chartered as a town in 1730 when it was set off from Providence. The early settlers were predominantly Quakers. In 1871, some of Smithfield's territory was ceded to Woonsocket and the rest split into three municipalities: Smithfield, North Smithfield and Lincoln. Smithfield is home to Bryant University and many apple orchards.

South Kingstown (29,277): Scene of the 1675 Great Swamp Fight, the key battle in King Philip's War, Kings Town was divided into north and south in 1722. South Kingstown is composed of a number of villages including Peace Dale, Wakefield and Kingston (home to the

TAKE 5 TOP FIVE OUTRAGEOUS
NEWPORT MANSIONS

1. **The Breakers**. The ultimate Newport "cottage," the Italian Renaissance-inspired 130,000 square foot Breakers has 70 rooms and was commissioned by Cornelius Vanderbilt in the 1890s. The Great Hall is nearly 50 feet high, and the wrought iron gates outside weigh seven tons.

2. **The Elms**. Modeled on an actual French chateau, the Elms was built in 1901 for Pennsylvania coal barons. The large grounds include elaborate Classical Revival gardens.

3. **Chateau-Sur-Mer**. Completed in 1852, the original High Victorian design is understated relative to the competition. One of the earlier mansions, it was famous for its grand entertainments and parties.

4. **Rosecliff**. Completed in 1902 for the heir to a Nevada silver fortune, Rosecliff was used as a location for the 1974 film *The Great Gatsby*. The opulent residence features a Court of Love inspired by Marie Antoinette's Chateau de Versailles.

5. **Marble House**. Another Vanderbilt place, this one completed in 1892 for William Vanderbilt. Marble House features massive exterior Corinthian columns, a 10-ton 16 by 25 foot grille on the front entrance, and a "Gold Ballroom" shocking in its extravagance.

University of Rhode Island). The area has long represented the agricultural heartland of the state.

Tiverton (15,079): Tiverton was originally incorporated as part of the Massachusetts Bay Colony in 1694; it was transferred to Rhode Island and reincorporated in 1747. Popular with vacationers, Tiverton lies just south of Fall River, a Massachusetts city of 90,000 people.

Warren (11,083): Warren was named after Admiral Sir Peter Warren, a British naval war hero. The area was visited by Europeans as early as 1621, and served as a Plymouth Colony trading post in 1632. Roger Williams lived in the area briefly before settling in Providence in 1636. Warren was part of the town of Sowams which was incorporated in 1668 as part of Massachusetts, and subsequently transferred to Rhode Island in 1746.

Warwick (85,097): Rhode Island's second largest city was founded in 1642 by dissident and troublemaker Samuel Gorton who established himself in an area known as Shawomet. Soon after its founding, the settlement was the subject of fierce battles involving the Massachusetts Bay Colony and Indian tribes. The city was named in honor of the Earl of Warwick who granted it an official charter in 1647. Warwick lost a good part of its territory to Coventry in 1741 and West Warwick in 1913, and was incorporated as a city in 1931. Following WWII, suburban Warwick exhibited spectacular population growth. Warwick is home to Goddard State Park, T.F. Green State Airport, the Community College of Rhode Island's Knight Campus and more big box retailers and malls than you can shake a stick at.

Did you know. . .

that the towns of Richmond, Wisconsin (founded 1841, pop. 2,000) and Woonsocket, South Dakota (founded 1883, pop. 650) were named after their Rhode Island counterparts?

TAKE 5 CHRISTOPHER MARTIN'S TOP FIVE
RHODE ISLAND ODDBALL ATTRACTIONS

Christopher Martin grew up in Woodstock, New York, and has lived in Rhode Island for twenty years. A resident of Johnston, he is Editor-in-Chief of quahog.org, an exhaustively researched site that details the culture, history and attractions of the Ocean State. Quahog.org was voted "Best Local Website" in *Rhode Island Monthly*'s 2008 readers' poll, and leaves no hot weiner unturned in its mission to be "the definitive Rhode Island road trip."

1. **Musée Patamécanique**, undisclosed location, Bristol. Art, mechanics and museology come together in a series of ten bizarre exhibits curated by artist Neil Salley. Tours by appointment only.

2. **Florence Nightingale's nurse cap**, Westerly Hospital lobby, Westerly. The Angel of the Crimea, whose pioneering work in nursing, sanitation, and statistics let to dramatically improved hospital conditions and saved thousands of lives, never visited the United States. So why is one of her hats on display in Westerly? Stop by and find out. Open 24 hours.

3. **The Prinster Hogg Memorial**, Crazy Corners, Scituate. A large boulder commemorates the pilots (pilot Thomas N. Prinster and co-pilot Lyle W. Hogg) who made an emergency landing of their burning passenger plane on the frozen Scituate Reservoir in February 1982. The commuter flight had been en-route from Groton, Connecticut to Boston when a fire broke out in the cockpit and spread to the cabin. There were a number of serious injuries, including major burns to the pilots, and one passenger died. The Memorial is open dawn to dusk.

4. **German submarine U-853**, under 130 feet of water, east of Block Island. Only experienced divers should attempt to visit this attraction, a WWII German patrol sub that was sunk by American naval forces on May 7, 1945, just hours before Germany signed surrender papers and ended the war. In addition to the 55 crew members entombed in the wreck, at least four divers have lost their lives while visiting the sub since 1953.

5. **Grave of John Rogers Vinton**, Swan Point Cemetery, Providence. Vinton's grave is topped by the very cannonball that killed him during the Battle of Vera Cruz, Mexico, on March 22, 1847. Viewable during regular cemetery hours.

West Greenwich (6,394): In 1709, 35,000 acres known as the "vacant lands" west of East Greenwich were purchased by a group of thirteen men. In 1741, West Greenwich was set off from East Greenwich and incorporated. The town features large expanses of protected land including Arcadia State Park and Big River Management Area.

West Warwick (29,289): West Warwick was born in 1913 when it split from Warwick; despite being nearly 100 years old, it qualifies as Rhode Island's youngest town. West Warwick is comprised of six villages, and its many Pawtuxet River mills made it a leading center for textile production in the nineteenth and early twentieth centuries.

Westerly (23,408): Westerly was incorporated in 1669 and is in Rhode Island's southwestern corner on the Connecticut border; it got its name from this location. Westerly is known for its quarries and lovely beaches, notably Watch Hill which has a famous lighthouse of the same name. Westerly was hard hit by the 1938 hurricane which killed many and permanently altered the coast. Downtown Westerly is home to the elegant Wilcox Park.

Woonsocket (43,590): Woonsocket is the sixth largest city in the state; its name is derived from the Indian "thundermist." The area was claimed by Europeans as early as the 1660s. Thanks to its key Blackstone River location and accompanying falls, a series of mill villages developed beginning in 1810. The area reached its apex in the mid and late 1800s when the Providence & Worcester Railroad served the many booming textile mills. The city of Woonsocket was formed in 1888, uniting six villages which previously had belonged to Cumberland and Smithfield. Woonsocket's Main Street is home to many historic buildings, including several vintage mills.

People

Rhode Island was a multicultural society long before the word came into the language. For millennia, several Indian tribes inhabited the area around Narragansett Bay, either permanently or as a spot for trading, hunting and fishing. Giovanni da Verrazano's 1524 voyage was the first recorded instance of European contact, but the first European settlement wasn't until the 1630s when religious dissidents from neighbouring Massachusetts established themselves in the area. Rhode Island soon became known for its openness and tolerance, and in its early days accepted Jews and Quakers, two much persecuted groups of the time.

Less impressively, in the 1600s and 1700s, thousands of Africans were brought to Rhode Island as slaves, although by the late eighteenth century most of them had been freed. In the early 1800s, the Irish became Rhode Island's first traditional immigrant group; they were followed by newcomers from Quebec and a number of European countries. A 1965 change to US law increased non-European immigration, and the vast majority of current Rhode Island immigrants are from Latin America, Asia and Africa.

RACE IN RHODE ISLAND

White	88.7 percent
Black/African American	6.3 percent
American Indian/Alaskan Native	0.6 percent
Asian	2.6 percent
Two or more races	1.5 percent

The Hispanic or Latino category represents 11.2 percent of the Rhode Island population, but is not considered a racial group.

Source: US Census Bureau.

ANCESTRY

The following are Rhode Island's leading ancestries (multiple ancestries are possible).

Italian	19.0 percent
Irish	18.4 percent
English	12.0 percent
French	10.9 percent
Portuguese	8.7 percent
French Canadian	6.4 percent
German	5.3 percent
Polish	4.1 percent

Source: US Census Bureau.

COMING TO AMERICA

12.6 percent of Rhode Island's population is foreign born, second in New England to Massachusetts where 14.4 percent of the population is comprised of immigrants. Providence County ranks fourth among New England counties with 17.3 percent of its population born abroad.

PERCENTAGE OF POPULATION BORN ABROAD

Year	Rhode Island	New England	US
2005	12.6	11.5	12.4
1990	9.5	7.9	7.9
1950	14.4	13.9	6.9
1900	31.4	25.8	13.6
1850	16.2	11.2	9.7

Source: US Census Bureau.

TOP 10 COUNTRIES OF ORIGIN OF
RHODE ISLAND IMMIGRANTS (2007)

"Immigrants" refers to those granted legal permanent residency in the US during the fiscal year.

Dominican Republic	657
Guatemala	346
Cape Verde	290
Columbia	189
Liberia	140
China	115
Haiti	111
India	104
Cambodia	84
Nigeria	81

Source: US Citizen and Immigration Services.

Did you know. . .

that Touro Synagogue in Newport was one of the stops on the Underground Railroad traversed by southern Blacks on their way to freedom in the north and Canada? The building was vacant in the mid-1800s, and its Quaker caretaker allowed escaped slaves to stay there.

TALKING THE TALK

Four-fifths of Rhode Islanders five years of age and older speak only English at home; the remaining 200,000 or so speak another tongue, although they may speak English as well. Of people speaking languages other than English, Spanish speakers comprise nearly half. The breakdown of non-English speakers is as follows:

- Spanish or Spanish Creole: 47 percent
- Portuguese or Portuguese Creole: 18.0 percent
- French or French Creole: 9.8 percent
- Italian: 4.9 percent
- Mon-Khmer, Cambodian: 2.4 percent
- Laotian: 2.0 percent

Source: US Census Bureau.

THE UNITED NATIONS OF PROVIDENCE

According to the US Census Bureau, 29 percent of the city of Providence's population was born outside the United States, and over 46 percent of the population five years of age and older speaks a language other than English at home. The city is also racially diverse — the White share is 48.5 percent, Black/African American, 15.0 percent; Asian, 5.9 percent; and the elusive "some other race," 26.2 percent. People of Hispanic or Latino origin (of any race) represent 36 percent of Providence's population.

NATIVE PEOPLES

When the European colonists arrived, the Narragansett and Wampanoag were the major Indian tribes occupying present day Rhode Island. The Wampanoag were in the East Bay (their reach extended east to Cape Cod and the islands of Nantucket and Martha's Vineyard) while the Narragansett were on the west side of the Bay and in western Rhode Island.

Relations were generally good between Rhode Island founder Roger Williams and local Aboriginals. Leaders of other nearby colonies, however, weren't nearly so enlightened as Williams and grabbed greater and greater amounts of Native-occupied land. The uneasy coexistence between Natives and Colonists came to a head in King Philip's War in 1675-76, a series of skirmishes and battles that devastated the local Indian population. Many Natives were killed in the fighting, some were captured and sold as slaves, and others left the area in the wake of the conflict. The Narragansett were confined to an area of Charlestown where the Niantic tribe had been granted land, and the two tribes effectively merged under the Narragansett name. Over time, much of the initial reservation was sold to pay debts, or was simply taken.

The State of Rhode Island "detribalized" the Narragansett in the 1880s, effectively liquidating the tribe. The Narragansett continued to function, however, electing leaders, and even incorporating in 1934. In 1975, the tribe sued the state and local landowners for the return of 3,200 acres of Charlestown land, settling for 1,800 acres in a 1978 out-of-court agreement. The tribe has been recognized by the federal government since 1983, although it has been thwarted in its attempts to sell tax-free cigarettes on tribal land, or to gain authorization to operate a casino.

Rhode Island's American Indian/Alaskan Native population is about 6,350 people, or 0.06 percent of the state total. The Narragansett Indian Tribe numbers 2,400 people, most of whom live in Rhode Island. Tribe members are linked genealogically to the 1880-84 Rolls used at the time of detribalization.

AFRICAN AMERICAN RHODE ISLAND

Africans were first brought to Rhode Island as slaves as early as the 1650s. Their numbers increased substantially in the 1700s, and a 1770 census recorded 30 percent of Newport's population as African American. In the 1700s, many African Americans, both enslaved and free, worked on South County plantations; others were employed in maritime trades and as skilled craftsmen. African Americans were employed in building some of Rhode Island's most famous buildings including Touro Synagogue and Redwood Library in Newport, and John Brown House in Providence. In

TAKE 5 FIVE AFRICAN AMERICAN RHODE ISLANDERS

1. **George Wiley (1931-1973)**. Warwick-raised Wiley received a bachelor's degree from URI, and a Ph.D. in chemistry from Cornell. He taught at several universities, but left academia in 1964 to work on social and racial justice issues. Wiley founded the Poverty/Rights Action Center and the National Welfare Rights Organization. He died in a 1973 boating accident, and the Pawtucket based anti-poverty organization The George Wiley Center is named in his honor.

2. **Paul Gaines (1932-)**. Newport-born Gaines was elected that city's only African American mayor in 1981. A long time administrator at Bridgewater State College in Massachusetts, Gaines spearheaded the creation of the Portsmouth monument to the Rhode Island Black Regiment.

3. **Michael S. Van Leesten (1943-)**. A veteran of 1960s-era civil rights activism, Rhode Island College grad Van Leesten is head of the Van Leesten Group, a Providence firm specializing in real estate, commercial and community development. Van Leesten chairs the Providence Black Repertory Company, and has served as Executive Director of the Providence Planning and Development Department, and as Chairman of the Rhode Island Home Mortgage & Finance Corporation.

4. **Ruth Simmons (1945-)**. The Texas-born Simmons was the youngest of 12 children; her mother was a maid and her father a sharecropper and factory worker. She was named Brown University's eighteenth president in 2001, becoming the first African American to head an Ivy League institution. Simmons, who has a Ph.D. in Romance literature from Harvard, was previously president of Smith College, and has held senior positions at Spelman College and Princeton University.

5. **Ojetta Rogeriee Thompson (1951-)**. Thompson, a Brown University grad, was nominated in April 2009 to serve as judge on the 1st US Circuit Court of Appeals. Thompson was the first African American woman to serve on the Rhode Island Superior Court. Her brother-in-law is Superior Court judge Edward C. Clifton, whose1979 appointment to the Providence Municipal Court made him the first African American appointed to any court in the state.

1784, the gradual emancipation law was passed, although the importation of slaves had been banned a decade earlier.

African American Rhode Islanders were an integral part of the colony's early life, and even formed the First Rhode Island Regiment, or Black Regiment, during the Revolutionary War. The Black Regiment, which fought in the battle of Rhode Island, was disbanded in 1783, its members receiving their freedom, but little else, for their service.

In the 1800s, many African Americans in South County moved north to Providence. They lived in segregated neighbourhoods which would become the scene of race riots in 1824 and 1831. In the mid-1800s, despite the mass immigration of people to the northern part of the state to work in Rhode Island's booming factories, most African Americans were denied such employment and often toiled as labourers, janitors or domestic workers.

Rhode Island's current Black population numbers about 55,000, roughly half of whom live in the city of Providence. While some African American Rhode Islanders are the descendants of slaves brought to the colony hundreds of years ago, many others came to Rhode Island much later, arriving in the early 1900s and later as part of the Great Migration of African Americans from the South to the northern cities.

Black Rhode Island has also historically included a substantial Cape Verdean community, and since the 1970s the state has received a number of immigrants from continental Africa. Providence is home to one of the United States' largest communities of people from Liberia, a country of 3.5 million people on the west coast of Africa. Some of these immigrants' ancestors may even be Rhode Islanders; in the 1800s, a number of the state's most prominent African Americans emigrated to Liberia, which was established by freed American slaves in 1822.

Did you know...

that Allan Fung's November 2008 election as Cranston mayor made him Rhode Island's first mayor of Asian descent?

TAKE 5 SCOTT MOLLOY'S FIVE
IRISH AMERICAN RHODE ISLAND PIONEERS

Scott Molloy, a labor historian at the Schmidt Labor Research Center at the University of Rhode Island, helped bring to fruition a million dollar Irish Famine Memorial in Providence in 2007. A former RIPTA bus driver, he is author of several books including *Trolley Wars: Streetcar Workers on the Line* (2007) and *All Aboard: The History of Mass Transportation in Rhode Island* (2004). His most recent publication, *Irish Titan, Irish Toilers: Joseph Banigan and Nineteenth Century New England Labor* (UNH Press, 2008) traces the early history of the Irish in the Ocean State. Irish Catholics began arriving in the 1820s with agricultural skills rather than those demanded by an industrial society, and faced prejudice and discrimination lasting well into the twentieth century. Eventually, they overcame these obstacles and became the state's largest ethnic group, filling virtually every vocational niche.

1. **Joseph Banigan, (1837-1898)**. Banigan was born in County Monaghan, Ireland, escaped the potato blight and came to Rhode Island in 1847 with his family. A full-time child laborer at age nine (he had one year of elementary school education), Banigan displayed an entrepreneurial pluck more reflective of local Yankees. He schooled himself in the emerging rubber footwear industry, and built a boot and shoe empire in Woonsocket by employing his own kind. He became the president of the United States Rubber Company in 1894, and was a decorated philanthropist to the Catholic Church.

2. **John J. Fitzgerald (1871-1926)**. Fitzgerald was one of the first Irish-Catholics to graduate from Brown University, receiving his diploma in 1893. He earned a law degree at Georgetown University, and in 1900 was elected mayor of Pawtucket on a populist platform. He unabashedly supported blue collar ethnics in the state, and became a riveting figure in the local Democratic Party. Fitzgerald formed a dynamic law partnership with his close friend James H. Higgins, and orchestrated Higgins's election as the first Irish-Catholic governor of Rhode Island in 1907. Fitzgerald vibrantly championed Irish independence, particularly in resolutions at Democratic Party national conventions.

3. **Patrick J. McCarthy (1848-1921)**. McCarthy was another youthful refugee from the Great Irish Famine. Orphaned by the vagaries of hunger and disease, he managed to graduate from Harvard Law School in 1868. He subsequently entered Rhode Island politics, serving in many different capacities. He curried the support of his Irish countrymen, and in 1907-08 became the only immigrant mayor in Providence history. His daughter published his memoirs, and McCarthy made a final plea for the Irish on his own tombstone inscription, an Irish Cross in Pawtucket's St. Francis Cemetery.

4. **Patrick T. Conley (1938-)**. Conley grew up in working class South Providence. He attended local Catholic schools and secured a prestigious scholarship to Notre Dame University. After graduating with a Ph.D., he joined the faculty at Providence College where he taught American History as well as a course about Rhode Island and its Hibernian past. Dr. Conley became the most prolific writer in the state's legendary pantheon of writers. Although he specializes in constitutional history, he paid homage to his Irish ancestors in his other writings and lectures. He is also a lawyer and businessman who has championed the redevelopment of the Providence Harbor. As president of the Rhode Island Heritage Hall of Fame, he nominated and inducted worthy predecessors from the Old Sod who had been previously overlooked.

5. **Arlene Violet (1943-)**. Violet also grew up in the urban quarters of South Providence. She came from a politically active Irish family in the Republican Party, an unusual affiliation in this Democratically-dominant ward. She joined the Sisters of Mercy and became a social activist in the Order, often marching on behalf of Cesar Chavez' Farm Workers Union and other social causes. She later turned to electoral politics. In 1984 she became the first female Attorney General in the country and established a reputation for unbridled fairness. She fearlessly fought crime, particularly within the ranks of government itself. Following her political career, she entered the field of talk radio, enjoying blazing success as an Irish-American female pioneer once again.

JEWISH RHODE ISLAND

Jewish Rhode Islanders number about 19,000, just under two percent of the state's population. Rhode Island represents one of North America's oldest Jewish settlements, with several Jewish families having established themselves in Newport in the late 1650s. Moreover, Newport's Touro Synagogue, which was completed in 1763, is the oldest existing synagogue in the US, and the nation's longest extant Jewish Cemetery is the 1677-established Hebrew Cemetery on Bellevue Avenue.

The state's earliest Jews came to Rhode Island from the West Indies (having earlier fled Europe), and in the mid 1700s, a number of Spanish and Portuguese Sephardic Jews settled in Newport. Some of these Jewish pioneers enjoyed substantial commercial success and were prominent local citizens; however, the community waned in the late eighteenth century. Rhode Island Jewry was revitalized in the mid-1800s when Jews from Germany and Central Europe arrived. In the 1880s, when pogroms in Poland and Russian produced an exodus of Jews to North America, a Yiddish speaking community established itself in Providence.

Rhode Island's Jewish community is currently served by a number of synagogues, as well as the Jewish Federation of Rhode Island and the Jewish Community Center of Rhode Island. Just over half of Rhode Island's Jewish population is either a member of a synagogue or a Jewish organization.

THE IRISH

Irish immigrants first came to Rhode Island in substantial numbers in the 1820s, although there had been an Irish presence in the state as early as the 1700s. Many of the Irish newcomers of the 1820s worked in mills, or in building railroads and the Blackstone Canal.

Land reforms in 1830s Ireland impoverished many peasants, and a devastating 1840s famine resulted in major Irish immigration to North America. Rhode Island's Irish population swelled, such that by the 1860s the Irish were far and away the dominant immigrant group. As light skinned English speakers, the Irish hardly seem "ethnic" at all; however,

Rhode Island-born Yankee Protestants were suspicious of Catholics, and disdainful of the newcomers' lack of education and skills.

"Irish" is the second most widely reported ancestry among Rhode Islanders ("Italian" is first), and yearly Saint Patrick's Day parades are held in several cities including Providence, Pawtucket and Newport. There are many Irish pubs in the state, and plentiful Irish musicians, including Pendragon, who have been playing Celtic music around Rhode Island for over a quarter-century.

FRENCH CANADIANS

Québécois immigrants formed a major portion of Rhode Island textile mill employees during the industry's heyday in the late 1800s and early 1900s. Many Québécois left rural Quebec to work in New England mills and the Rhode Island cities of Woonsocket, Pawtucket, and West Warwick were among their principal destinations. At one time, Woonsocket was known as the most French city in America, and a sign on Main Street still reads "Bienvenu à Woonsocket."

The French Canadian immigrants of the 1800s were devout Catholics who came from rural Quebec and had little, if any, formal education. They impressed the mill bosses as hard workers who would toil long hours without complaint. Some were migrant workers who worked in the mills in the colder months and then returned to Quebec to farm in the summer.

Few Québécois spoke English, and French was routinely heard in the mills and on the streets of Woonsocket and other textile towns. Woonsocket had a French daily newspaper until the 1940s, and there were also regular French language radio broadcasts. Moreover, until the mid-1920s, many Rhode Island French Canadians were educated in French. The Québécois population was augmented by other French speaking immigrants from Belgium and France.

By the 1930s, the stream of newcomers from north of the border had effectively ended, the result of changes in US immigration law, the Depression and a falling Quebec birthrate.

TAKE 5 FIVE JEWISH RHODE ISLANDERS

1. **Frank Licht (1916-87)**. Licht, Rhode Island's first Jewish governor, was born in Providence and educated at Brown and Harvard. He held office from 1969 to 1973, previously having served as a state senator and Rhode Island Superior Court Judge. Bruce Sundlun, who served from 1991-95, was Rhode Island's second Jewish governor.

2. **Alan Shawn Feinstein (1931-)**. Businessman, writer, teacher and, since 1996, full-time philanthropist, Feinstein was born in Massachusetts but has lived in Cranston since the 1960s. His charitable efforts are well publicized, and he is particularly dedicated to alleviating hunger and promoting education and public service. Feinstein has received numerous awards, including honorary doctorates from most of Rhode Island's post-secondary institutions.

3. **Walter Mossberg (1947-)**. The technology guru for the technology leery, *Wall Street Journal* columnist and editor Mossberg is co-creator and producer of the WSJ's annual "D: All Things Digital" conference which brings together the movers and shakers in the tech industry. A personal technology columnist since 1991, Mossberg grew up in Warwick, graduating from Pilgrim High School in 1965. In 2001, he received an honorary doctorate of laws from the University of Rhode Island.

4. **Alan G. Hassenfeld (1949-)**. Hasbro Inc., Board Member and retired Chairman and CEO of the company. Hassenfeld started at Hasbro (which was founded by his grandfather in 1923) in 1970 following graduation from the University of Pennsylvania. From 1984 to 2003, in the roles of President, CEO and Chairman, he was vital in expanding Hasbro internationally and adding to the company's stock of brands. Hassenfeld serves in leadership positions on behalf of many Rhode Island non-profits, charities and foundations.

5. **Merrill W. Sherman (1949-)**. Sherman is President and CEO of Bancorp Rhode Island, Inc., and its subsidiary, Bank Rhode Island. She was behind Bank Rhode Island's 1996 creation, and has served as President and CEO of two other New England banks. Trained as a lawyer, Sherman is Chair of the RISD Board of Trustees and serves on the boards of a number of Rhode Island non-profits.

THE FABRE LINE

The Fabre Line was a Marseilles, France-based steamship company that docked in Providence from 1911 to 1934. It was a key element in the boom in southern European immigration to the state in the early 1900s.

Fabre Line ships would depart Marseilles and makes stops in southern and central Italy, followed by Sicily, Portugal, and the Azores Islands. It's no accident that people of Italian and Portuguese ancestry comprise a significant portion of Rhode Island's population. About 50,000 Italians came to Rhode Island in the first third of the twentieth century, as did 20,000 Portuguese nationals. The Fabre Line also had feeder ships in the 1920s, bringing immigrants from other parts of the Mediterranean and Middle East to Rhode Island.

At one point, Providence was the fifth largest landing port for immigrants to the US. Of course, not all of them stayed in Providence — some moved on to other parts of the country, and thousands of others returned home. Not all immigrants found the New World to their liking, and some used money earned in the US to better establish themselves in their homelands. The Fabre Line discontinued service to Providence in 1934, the result of 1920s immigration quotas and the Depression.

Did you know...

that one of Rhode Island's most celebrated artists, the African American landscape painter Edward M. Bannister (1828-1901), was born in St. Andrews, New Brunswick, Canada? Bannister moved to Boston as a young man and came to Providence in 1870 with his wife, a successful businesswoman. Bannister, winner of a medal at the 1876 Centennial Exposition in Philadelphia, was a founder of the Providence Art Club and taught at the Rhode Island School of Design.

TAKE 5 FIVE QUÉBÉCOIS
RHODE ISLANDERS

1. **Napoleon Lajoie (1875-1959)**. Lajoie was born in Woonsocket to immigrant parents. He is still considered one of the greatest hitters in baseball history, and was one of nine members of the baseball Hall of Fame's 1937 inaugural class.

2. **Aram Pothier (1854-1928)**. Pothier was born in Quebec and came to Rhode Island as a young man. Among other offices, Pothier was elected Woonsocket mayor, lieutenant governor of Rhode Island, and governor. Pothier served several terms as governor, first from 1909-15, and then later from 1925-28 (he died in office).

3. **Emery San Souci (1857-1936)**. San Souci, born in Maine to French Canadian parents, was a Providence department store owner who served as governor of Rhode Island from 1921-23. Previously, Sans Souci had been lieutenant governor, a Providence city council-man and a close aide of Aram Pothier during the latter's first tenure as governor.

4. **Ben Mondor (1925-)**. Quebec-born Ben Mondor was raised in Woonsocket and is a graduate of Mount St. Charles Academy. He was in the textile business for many years, but is best known locally for purchasing the Pawtucket Red Sox in 1977 and transforming the team into one of baseball's most successful minor league franchises. He is a member of the Boston Red Sox Hall of Fame, and received an honorary doctorate from Rhode Island College.

5. **David Plante (1940-)**. Novelist and memoirist Plante, the son of immigrant parents, grew up in Providence speaking French and attending Catholic schools taught by Québécois nuns. He is a professor of creative writing at Columbia University, and the author of over a dozen books including *American Ghosts* (2005), a memoir about his Providence boyhood. He has won numerous awards for his work, which often deals with homosexuality and his French Canadian immigrant background.

ITALIAN RHODE ISLAND

Probably no immigrant group is more associated with Rhode Island than Italians. About 200,000 people, or nineteen percent of the state's population, claim Italian ancestry, a higher percentage than any other state. Rhode Island's most Italian areas include Johnston, North Providence, Cranston and Providence's Silver Lake neighbourhood.

Most Italian immigrants came to the state between 1890 and 1940, in some cases effectively resettling their native towns on this side of the Atlantic; the strong link between Cranston's Knightsville district and Itri is one example. Some Italian immigrants of the early 1900s were masons and stonecutters who settled near granite quarries around Westerly; others found work on farms or in Providence area factories, and some became peddlers, merchants and small businessmen.

Federal Hill, an area west of downtown Providence, is Rhode Island's Little Italy and in the first half of the twentieth century was almost exclusively Italian. Previously, it had been a mostly Irish enclave. These days, you're more likely to hear Spanish spoken than Italian on Federal Hill streets, although Atwells Avenue with its

Did you know. . .

that the Berlitz language school empire was launched in the 1870s on Westminster Street in Providence? The school was started by German immigrant David Berliztheimer who had come to the US in 1870 and changed his name to Maximillian Berlitz. His philosophy of immersing the learner in the target language evolved more or less by chance: Berlitz's sole initial employee, a Frenchman called Nicholas Joly, spoke no English and in Berlitz's absence taught students by pointing at objects and acting out verbs. The method proved a success, and in the 1880s Berlitz schools opened in Boston, New York and Washington DC. The famed Berlitz method was even demonstrated at World Fairs in Paris in 1900 and St. Louis in 1904.

TAKE 5 FIVE ITALIAN AMERICAN RHODE ISLAND POLITICIANS

1. **John O. Pastore (1907-2000)**. Providence-born Pastore was Rhode Island's first Italian American governor (1945-50), and its first Italian American US senator (1950-76).
2. **Christopher Del Sesto (1907-1973)**. Providence-born Del Sesto served as governor from 1959-61.
3. **John A. Notte, Jr. (1909-1983)**. Providence-born Notte served as governor from 1961-63.
4. **Edward DiPrete (1934-)**. Cranston-born DiPrete served as governor from 1985-91.
5. **Buddy Cianci (1941-)**. Cranston-born Cianci served as Providence mayor from 1975-84 and 1991-2002.

dozens of Italian restaurants, markets and shops retains a special place in the hearts of Italian (and non Italian) Rhode Islanders.

There are plenty of parades, feasts, processions and festivals to keep Italian Rhode Islanders in touch with their roots. Many of these events are sponsored by local Catholic churches. St. Joseph's Day, celebrated on March 19, is a biggie, and one on which the consumption of zeppole (a cream-filled puff pastry dusted with powdered sugar) is more or less mandatory.

PORTUGUESE RHODE ISLAND

There has been a Portuguese presence in Rhode Island since the 1600s. An early success story was Aaron Lopez, a Sephardic Jew, who was born in Lisbon in 1731 and came to Newport in the early 1750s. He owned numerous sailing ships and was one of the founders of Touro Synagogue, the nation's oldest.

A major wave of Portuguese Rhode Islanders came to the US in the mid 1800s, and were engaged in whaling (Bristol and Warren were major whaling centers) as well as fishing and other maritime pursuits. Later immigrants were more likely to be agricultural and factory workers.

Rhode Island has a higher percentage of residents of Portuguese ancestry than any other state. Within Rhode Island, Cumberland, East Providence and Bristol have particularly large Portuguese populations, and the region encompassing metro Providence, the East Bay and southeastern Massachusetts represents the largest concentration of Lusophones in the country.

Only some Portuguese Rhode Islanders are from mainland Portugal, many hail from the Atlantic Ocean archipelago of the Azores, or the island of Madeira. Rhode Island also has historically been home to a sizeable number of people from Cape Verde, a former Portuguese colony (independent since 1975) which lies several hundred miles off the coast of Africa.

Rhode Islanders of Portuguese descent include retired US Rhode Island District Court Senior Judge Ernest Torres, *Today* co-anchor and East Providence native Meredith Vieira, Bristol-born pro golfer Billy Andrade, and storyteller Len Cabral of Providence, a Cape Verdean Rhode Islander.

Did you know. . .

that Tavares, the smooth singing quintet that garnered a hit in the late 1970s with "More than a Woman" from the *Saturday Night Fever* soundtrack are Cape Verdean Rhode Islanders? Tavares (comprised of brothers Pooch, Ralph, Tiny, Chubby and Butch Tavares) also scored several other chart successes and are still performing. The Grammy Award winners grew up in the Fox Point section of Providence, as well as in New Bedford, Massachusetts, and are members of the Cape Verdean Heritage Hall of Fame. Their father, Feliciano "Flash" Tavares (1920-2008), was also a well-known musician and singer.

LATINO RHODE ISLAND

Latinos are a fast growing ethnic bloc and represent about 11 percent of the Rhode Island population or roughly 120,000 people. Rhode Island ranks twelfth in the country in the percentage of its population that is of Hispanic origin, and the city of Providence's population is around one third Latino; Pawtucket also has a major Latino community, and the city of Central Falls is about half Latino.

Like immigrant groups before them, Latinos have transformed the landscape, and Hispanic markets, restaurants and clubs, as well as Catholic churches, are thriving in certain parts of the state.

Dominican Rhode Islanders first came to the state in the 1940s, and comprise an important share of the local Latino population. Other significant Hispanic communities include those hailing from the US territory of Puerto Rico, and the countries of Colombia, Guatemala and Mexico. While Latinos tend to be underrepresented politically, there are several well known Rhode Island Hispanic legislators, including Providence City Councillors Luis Aponte, Miguel Luna and Leon Tejada (who previously served in the Rhode Island House of Representatives). In the General Assembly, Anastasia Williams (born in 1957 in Panama) and Grace Diaz (born in 1957 in the Dominican Republic) are members of the House, while Juan Pichardo (born in 1966 in the Dominican Republic) is a State Senator.

Did you know...

that Rhode Island is the most Catholic state in the nation with 52 percent of its population so identifying itself? Rhode Island was not founded by Catholics, but its historic sources of immigrants — Ireland, Quebec, Italy, Portugal, and more recently, Latin America, are predominantly Catholic.

GAY RHODE ISLAND

Gay Rhode Islanders have likely been around since the state's founding, but didn't put on a parade until 1976 when 75 people marched through downtown Providence. The Providence police had attempted to prevent the march, which was the brainchild of local gay clergy, but a court order allowed it to go forward. Several decades later, the difference is dramatic; not only does the city authorize the small night-time parade, but David Cicilline, Providence's openly gay mayor, is often its marshal. And he's not the first to serve in that capacity — former mayor Buddy Cianci was also known as a friend to the gay community, going so far as to fly the rainbow flag over City Hall, and calling numbers at gay Bingo night.

The number of gay, lesbian and bisexual Rhode Islanders is estimated at 27,000, or about 2.6 percent of the state population. RI Pride holds a yearly PrideFest which includes a Triple Crown Pageant in which contestants vie for the titles of Ms. Lesbian, Mr. Gay and Miss Gay Rhode Island. Providence is considered a gay travel hot spot with over a dozen gay or gay friendly bars in and around the downtown area.

It has been illegal to discriminate on the basis of sexual orientation in Rhode Island since 1995, although the state does not grant marriage licenses to same-sex couples. It does, however, recognize the same-sex marriages performed in neighboring Massachusetts and Connecticut.

Did you know. . .

that the Pew Hispanic Center estimates that Rhode Island's population of unauthorized immigrants is between 20,000 and 40,000 people? The number of authorized foreign born persons is about 134,000.

Natural World

Rhode Island's most famous feature is water, notably its numerous Narragansett Bay and Atlantic coast beaches. From above, Narragansett Bay looks like a series of fissures running through the eastern part of the state producing a scattering of islands, coves and peninsulas. Providence sits at the top of the Bay, where several rivers converge.

Given that it comprises barely 1,000 square miles of land, Rhode Island features surprising topographical variation. The state's urban areas are on or near the coast, and hardwood forests, farms and tracts of suburban homes dominate the gently rolling uplands. As one proceeds inland, there are remarkably dense forests for such a populated region.

Rhode Island's southern coast features highly prized and endangered marshlands and tidal ponds. The state also boasts many fresh water rivers, reservoirs, lakes and ponds. There aren't any mountains to speak of in Rhode Island, although the state is by no means flat. Providence is composed of seven hills, and there are modest peaks throughout Rhode Island, particularly in the western part of the state.

Rhode Island is hardly uncharted territory, but it still possesses some relatively undisturbed natural areas. State parks and management areas are supplemented by thousands of acres protected by organizations like the Audubon Society of Rhode Island and The Nature Conservancy, as well as towns and land trusts.

RHODE ISLAND'S OFFICIAL NATURAL SYMBOLS

State bird: Rhode Island Red, a breed of chicken
State fish: Striped Bass
State flower: Violet
State fruit: Rhode Island Greening Apple
State rock: Cumberlandite
State mineral: Bowenite
State shell: Quahog
State tree: Red Maple

PHYSICAL SETTING

- Size: 1,214 square miles (1,045 of land)
- Distance north to south: 48 miles
- East to west: 37 miles
- Percentage of United States' total area: 0.03
- Percentage of New England's total area: 1.8
- Geographic center: Middle Road in East Greenwich
- Highest elevation: Jerimoth Hill (812 feet)
- Total miles of coastline: Over 400
- Number of islands: Over 30 (Prudence, Patience and Hope among them)

LONGITUDE AND LATITUDE

- Latitude: 41 degrees 30 minutes North
- Longitude: 71 degrees 30 minutes West

(This spot is near the URI campus in southern Rhode Island).

- Rhode Island is located at the same latitude as Portugal and northern Japan, and at the same longitude as Quito, Ecuador and Quebec City, Canada.

GEOLOGICAL ORIGINS

Rhode Island's geography has been shaped by the movement of the Earth's crust, erosion and glaciers. It's estimated that Rhode Island first became part of the North American land mass about 400 million years ago when the prehistoric island of Avalonia collided with North America, adding a strip to the northeastern coast that includes eastern Maine, eastern Massachusetts and all of Rhode Island. About 50 million years later, southern continents collided with North America and created a huge continent (called Pangaea) that comprised almost all of the Earth's land mass. Pangaea survived for 100 million years, but then a rift developed along the current continental shelf and a new continent, Africa, began to drift to the southeast.

As time passed, the great mountain ranges of New England eroded, the Earth grew colder and glaciers moved southward, bulldozing rock and silt as they did so. The glaciers reached their southern most extension about 14,000 years ago. As they melted, they left rock deposits, or moraines. The southernmost moraine formed a line that today crosses Block Island, Martha's Vineyard and Nantucket. A second later moraine runs through Watch Hill in Westerly, Rhode Island and Cape Cod.

NARRAGANSETT BAY

Narragansett Bay is a spectacularly beautiful estuary that contains more than 60 species of fish and shellfish. In addition to supporting a vibrant fishing industry, the Bay is a world famous playground for boaters and beachgoers, and a source of pride for Rhode Islanders, none of whom are more than a thirty-minute drive from the shore. Although the Bay is associated with Rhode Island, its preservation is heavily dependent on the 60 percent of its watershed which lies in Massachusetts.

Did you know...

that as of early 2009, the record for world's largest pumpkin was held by Scituate's Joseph Jutras? Jutras's 2007 behemoth checked in at 1,689 pounds and broke the 2006 record of 1,502 pounds held by fellow Rhode Islander Ronald Wallace of Coventry.

Narragansett Bay was at one time notoriously polluted, but with the demise of Rhode Island's textile, jewelry and plating industries, and improved industrial and sewage waste water treatment, water quality has improved considerably in the last 40 years. Discharges of copper, lead and other heavy metals have declined 96 percent in the last 30 years, and construction of a huge system of underground tunnels to catch storm water run-off has improved oxygen levels.

Still, high nitrogen discharges from sewage plants continue to promote plant growth that in summer can deprive fish of needed oxygen. Measures advocated to improve the Bay include sewage treatment upgrades to reduce nitrogen levels, the restoration of coastal wetlands and the removal of dams that block the passage of migrating fish like shad and alewife.

OYSTERS

When Native Americans first introduced Roger Williams to oysters, they were abundant in Narragansett Bay. Apponaug, the village surrounding Warwick City Hall, means "place of oysters," in the Narragansett language. By the mid-1800s, Rhode Island had 27 oyster companies that together leased 20 percent of the Bay to raise shellfish. Seed oysters from Connecticut and Maryland were regularly transplanted to local waters to improve harvests.

By the early twentieth century, however, pollution and urbanization caused a decline in oysters. An important habitat in the upper bay, Oyster Island, was filled in to create Fields Point, a Providence waterfront industrial area, and the 1938 hurricane dealt the oyster population a major blow by washing thousands of them ashore.

Today, oysters are making a modest comeback through aquaculture. In 2007, 30 oyster farms sold 2.6 million oysters, and the $1.6 million industry tripled in size from 2003 to 2007. In addition to commercial efforts, Roger Williams University is growing and distributing tens of thousands of oysters throughout Narragansett Bay.

TAKE 5 FIVE MOST POPULAR PARKS

1. **Roger Williams Park & Zoo:** 430 acres in Providence with the nation's third oldest zoo, a botanical garden, natural history museum, paddle boats, tennis courts, butterfly garden, merry-go-round and walking trails.

2. **Lincoln Woods State Park:** 627 wooded acres in Lincoln with freshwater swimming, fishing, horseback riding, kayaking, picnicking and ball fields.

3. **Colt State Park:** 464 acres in Bristol with boat ramp, fishing, panoramic views of Narragansett Bay and 4 miles of jogging trails. Connected to the East Bay Bicycle Path.

4. **Goddard Memorial State Park:** 489 acres in Warwick including a saltwater beach, a nine-hole golf course, large open lawns, 81 tree species and 18 miles of bridal paths.

5. **Fort Adams State Park:** 105 acres in Newport harbor with two boat -ramps, salt water swimming, the Museum of Yachting and famous jazz and folk festivals.

Block Island

With 17 miles of beaches, 25 miles of trails, and more than 70 species of migratory song birds, Block Island is a haven for nature lovers.

Located 12 miles off Rhode Island's southern coast, Block Island marks the southern terminus of a glacier that receded 14,000 years ago. As it melted, the glacier left moraines, or scrap piles of rock and sand, from as far away as Canada; these now form Block Island and other New England coastal islands.

Block Island, which measures about 11 square miles, has retained much of its natural character thanks to the work of the state of Rhode Island, the US government, The Nature Conservancy and several local conservation groups. Forty-four percent of the island's land is currently protected, and there are walking trails sprinkled amongst its beaches, meadows and scrubland. Located along the Atlantic Flyway, the island is a stop-over for many migratory birds; every spring, special efforts are made to protect the beach nests of the diminutive and threatened piping plover.

Among the island's top natural areas is the 2.5 mile long Crescent Beach, which is within walking distance of the ferry. The Block Island National Wildlife Refuge sits at the island's northern tip, and features sandy beaches, a pond and a lighthouse. Nearby is Clay Head, a bluff with three miles of trails. At the other end of the island, Southeast Lighthouse provides views from high on the Monhegan Bluffs. The 230-acre Rodman's Hollow, a glacial outwash basin, also sits on the island's southern end and includes numerous trails. Hikers are encouraged to wear long pants and socks to fend off deer ticks which carry Lyme disease. Deer, misguidedly introduced to the island in the 1960s, are just one of the threats to Block Island's environmental health. While preservation efforts continue, luxury second home development, over-use, and pesticides continue to damage the island's ecology. The island has a year-round population of about 1,000 people, and a seasonal count of ten times that number.

Access to Block Island is primarily by ferry, with links to Long Island, NY, New London, CT and Newport and Point Judith in Rhode Island. Although cars and mopeds are allowed on the island, foot and bike transportation are encouraged.

TAKE5 TOP FIVE MOST COMMON
TREE SPECIES

1. **Red maple**
2. **Eastern white pine**
3. **Northern red oak**
4. **Black oak**
5. **Scarlet oak**

Sources: USDA Forest Service.

SALT PONDS

Coastal lagoons, otherwise known as salt ponds, are bodies of water that lie behind narrow bluffs and beaches; they are the gateway between fresh and salt water systems. The shallow ponds are rich in plants such as eelgrass, and are home to shellfish and other marine animals. They are also popular stopping places for migratory birds.

The ponds comprise 32 square miles and are found on both sides of Narragansett Bay, on Block Island and along the state's southern coast. This latter area is home to Point Judith Pond and Ninigret Pond, two of Rhode Island's better known coastal lagoons. Salt ponds are in a constant state of flux as erosion, sediment transport, rising tides and storms alter their physical characteristics and change the balance between salt and fresh water.

The health of Rhode Island's salt ponds is threatened by contami-

Did you know. . .

that Cumberlandite, Rhode Island's state rock, is a volcanic, slightly magnetic rock found almost exclusively on a four-acre lot in Cumberland? Cumberlandite is more than 1.5 billion years old, and is the product of a volcanic eruption that fused molten rock with two dozen different minerals. Fragments found on Block Island document the path of the Wisconsin Glacier.

Did you know...

that coal was mined in Portsmouth, Cranston and Cumberland during the nineteenth and early twentieth centuries? There are currently no coal mines in Rhode Island, and Rhode Island and Vermont are the only two states in the nation with no coal-fired power plants.

nated ground water, a product of increased construction and building in coastal areas. The biggest one-time menace to the ponds was a 1996 spill which dumped 820,000 gallons of home heating oil off the Rhode Island coast, harming aquatic birds, shellfish and lobsters. The non-profit Salt Ponds Coalition, as well as local, state and national government agencies, have been active in monitoring and protecting the health of Rhode Island's coastal lagoons.

TAKE 5 FIVE RHODE ISLAND NATURAL HAZARDS

1. **Mosquitoes**. Not only are the stinging pests annoying, Rhode Island mosquitoes can transmit West Nile Virus, a potentially serious illness. Late summer is the most dangerous time of year.
2. **Poison Ivy and Poison Oak**. These rash and itch producing plants are prevalent throughout Rhode Island.
3. **Ticks**. Deer ticks are found throughout the state, particularly in southern coastal areas. Tick bites can result in Lyme disease and other serious illnesses. Mid-summer is the most dangerous time of year.
4. **The water**. Every year, a number of inland and coastal Rhode Island beaches are closed due to high bacteria counts, often following heavy rains.
5. **The air.** Rhode Island, like much of the northeast US, experiences high ozone and fine particle pollutant levels. Each summer, the Department of Environment Management declares a number of Air Quality Alert days. In addition to human generated pollution, airborne tree, grass and weed allergens are common.

INLAND WATER

About 13 percent of Rhode Island's area is comprised of inland water including 357 freshwater ponds, lakes, and impoundments. The largest natural freshwater bodies are Watchaug Pond in Burlingame State Park in Charlestown, and Worden's Pond in the Great Swamp Management Area in South Kingstown. Rhode Island's largest body of freshwater, however, is the 3,390-acre Scituate Reservoir that supplies water to 60 percent of the state. Including five smaller reservoirs, the Scituate Reservoir system covers 4,563 acres and contains 41 billion gallons of water.

TAKE5 TOP FIVE
INVASIVE THREATS

These species did not evolve locally but instead have been transplanted by international trade. Due to their ability to reproduce rapidly and their lack of natural enemies, they commonly overwhelm native species and cause biological problems.

1. **Chinese Mitten Crab**. A hairy CD-sized freshwater crab that upsets the freshwater ecology and causes riverbank erosion by burrowing.

2. **Mile a Minute Vine**. A rapidly growing vine that smoothers native vegetation.

3. **Water Chestnut**. A prolific freshwater plant with underwater spikes that clog waterways.

4. **Asian Longhorned beetle**. A black beetle with white spots that bores into hardwood trees and kills them.

5. **Zebra mussels**. A fast reproducing shellfish that clogs water and sewer pipes.

Source: David Gregg, Executive Director of the Rhode Island Natural History Survey.

TAKE 5 TODD MCLEISH'S TOP FIVE
SPECIES OF RARE RHODE ISLAND WILDLIFE

Todd McLeish is a science writer at URI and the author of *Golden Wings and Hairy Toes: Encounters with New England's Most Imperiled Wildlife* (2007), and *Basking with Horseshoes: Tracking Threatened Marine Life in New England Waters* (2009). A resident of Burrillville, he has been writing about wildlife and environmental issues for 20 years.

1. **The American Burying Beetle**. The rarest beetle in North America, the American Burying Beetle is found almost exclusively on Block Island, where it feeds on the flesh of dead animals. Roger Williams Park Zoo in Providence is raising burying beetles in captivity for release on Nantucket and other islands to re-establish populations that previously existed there.

2. **The New England Cottontail**. Southern New England's only native rabbit, the New England Cottontail has nearly disappeared from the region and been replaced by its identical cousin, the introduced Eastern cottontail. Its last remaining strongholds in Rhode Island are a few scattered protected properties in the southern and western parts of the state.

3. **The Sandplain Gerardia**. New England's rarest plant, the Sandplain Gerardia is found primarily in historic cemeteries. The unusual species has tiny pink flowers and is closely related to foxgloves and snapdragons; Rhode Island's population is limited to one South County cemetery.

4. **The Ringed Boghaunter**. The first dragonfly to take flight in early spring, the Ringed Boghaunter emerges from sphagnum bogs to feed and breed in surrounding forests. Found in only a few dozen locations from southern Maine to eastern Connecticut, its healthiest populations are found in Richmond.

5. **The Eastern Spadefoot Toad**. The rarest amphibian in the region, the Eastern Spadefoot Toad lives in underground burrows in open forests or shrubland. The Eastern Spadefoot comes out to feed only after dark and is a homebody, rarely traveling more than 100 feet in its entire lifetime. The best place to find this secretive creature is in the watershed of the Wood River in Hopkinton and Richmond.

RIVERS . . .

- **Blackstone River:** The Blackstone powered America's Industrial Revolution, and is dotted with mill villages as well as larger centers like Woonsocket. It forms the centerpiece of the John H. Chafee Blackstone River Valley National Heritage Corridor, which includes small museums, parks and remnants of the Blackstone Canal. Beginning in Worcester, MA, the river heads south 46 miles before entering Narragansett Bay in Pawtucket.
- **Moshassuck River:** Most would call the Moshassuck a stream. It runs south ten miles from Lincoln to Providence, where it briefly joins the Woonasquatucket before entering Narragansett Bay.
- **Pawtuxet River:** The largest river contained in Rhode Island's borders, the Pawtuxet runs 16 miles east from urban Rhode Island's principle water source, the Scituate Reservoir, to Pawtuxet Cove on the Cranston/Warwick boundary.

TAKE 5 TOP FIVE RHODE ISLAND HIKING TRAILS

1. **The North South Trail:** 77 miles from the Atlantic Ocean to Massachusetts.
2. **The Cliff Walk:** 3.5 miles amidst Newport's coastline and opulent mansions.
3. **The Ben Utter Trail:** 3.4 mile loop trail in Exeter's Arcadia Management Area.
4. **The Vin Gormley Trail:** 8 mile loop trail in Charlestown's Burlingame State Park.
5. **The Walkabout Trail:** Three loop trails of 8, 6 and 2 miles in Glocester's George Washington Management Area.

- **Wood-Pawcatuck River:** The bucolic Wood-Pawcatuck features 55 miles of the best canoeing in Rhode Island. It begins in the sparsely populated center of Rhode Island, and heads south, forming the southwest border with Connecticut before emptying into the Atlantic Ocean.
- **Woonasquatucket River:** Starting in North Smithfield, the Woonasquatucket travels 19 miles, some of them through dense residential areas, before flowing under the Providence Place Mall and into Narragansett Bay.

TAKE 5 FIVE RHODE ISLAND
ENDANGERED PLANTS

1. **Eastern prickly pear cactus**. Related to its better-known western cousin, the eastern prickly pear cactus lives in sandy coastal habitats. Only one known site remains in Rhode Island, although the species has numerous other sites elsewhere in New England.

2. **New England boneset**. A 3-foot-tall plant with only 16 known sites in the world, six of which are in Rhode Island and ten in Massachusetts. It lives on the shores of kettle ponds, which are spring-fed ponds created by retreating glacial ice.

3. **Violet wood sorrel**. A native of semi-shaded woods, it is losing its habitat to suburban home development and denser forests. The violet wood sorrel has difficulty spreading because no animal eats its seeds. The plant has only four sites remaining in Rhode Island, and fewer than 20 in New England.

4. **Lizard's tail**. Among the most primitive of flowering plants, the 2.5 foot tall lizard's tail has only one known site in Rhode Island and three others in New England. It lives in freshwater wetlands and has a showy spike of white flowers.

5. **Yellow fringed orchid**. The plant's tall yellow flower is pollinated by butterflies and hummingbirds. It can grow up to 3 feet tall in moist sandy open areas, but has only two remaining sites in Rhode Island and eight others in New England.

Source: Hope Lesson, Rhode Island Natural History Society botanist.

RHODE ISLAND'S PERCENTAGE OF FORESTED LAND

1767: 36
1908: 38
1935: 62
1962: 68
1985: 65
2006: 55

Sources: The Rhode Island Atlas and USDA Forest Service.

FARM COUNTRY

Rhode Island farms occupy 61,000 acres.

- Number of farms: 868
- Number of farmers' markets: 36
- Percentage of farmland protected by the state: 10
- Percentage of farm income from greenhouses and nurseries: 67
- Percentage of farm income from fruits and vegetables: 14
- Percentage of farm income from livestock and poultry: 11
- Percentage of farm income from milk: 4

Source: Rhode Island Division of Agriculture.

Did you know...

that the University of Rhode Island's Graduate School of Oceanography operates a 185-foot research vessel called *The Endeavor*? The National Science Foundation owns the ship and uses it to carry out government-sponsored research and train graduate students. In addition to periodic cruises about Narragansett Bay, the ship has gone as far afield as the Black Sea, the Mediterranean Sea and the environs of the Easter and Galapagos Island in the South Pacific.

Weather

Rhode Island is blessed, or cursed, with a "moist continental climate," which means that much of the time it's too wet, too hot, or too cold. Still, compared to northern New England or the upper Midwest, Rhode Island's winters are mild. Similarly, Rhody summers, despite some uncomfortably humid days, are temperate relative to many areas of the country.

A hallmark of Rhode Island's weather is its changeability — the state's coastal location at the intersection of several storm tracks means that the weather can shift abruptly. There's also considerable variability within the state, particularly in winter. The difference between the mild southeast coast and the colder, snowier northwest part of the state can be striking, even though the two areas are separated by a mere 30 or so miles.

And while it might not be the Dakotas or the Mississippi Gulf, Rhode Island is prone to severe weather events. The state has been struck by hurricanes and blizzards, and those of a certain age love to bend youngsters' ears with tales of the "Blizzard of '78."

AT A GLANCE

- **Warmest month:** July (82.6° F average maximum; 64.1° F average minimum, 73.3° F daily average).
- **Coldest month:** January (37.1° F average maximum; 20.3° F average minimum, 28.7° F daily average).

- **Snowiest Months:** January (9.9 in. mean snowfall) and February (9.8 in. mean snowfall). The greatest accumulation of snow on the ground is typically between January 24 and February 12.
- **Highest recorded official temperature:** 104° F at Providence on August 2, 1975.
- **Lowest recorded official temperature:** -23° F at Kingston on January 11, 1942.

*Readings taken at T.F. Green Airport unless indicated otherwise.

Sources: National Oceanic & Atmospheric Administration; Northeast Regional Climate Center.

WINTER AND SUMMER TEMPERATURES AROUND NEW ENGLAND

Daily average February and August temperatures in degrees Fahrenheit

Bridgeport, CT	30.4	73.1
Hartford, CT	27.5	71.6
Providence,RI	**29.7**	**71.3**
Boston, MA	30.3	71.9
Worcester, MA	24.8	68.0
Concord, NH	21.8	67.3
Burlington, VT	18.2	67.9
Portland, ME	23.3	67.3

Source: Northeast Regional Climate Center.

LET THERE BE LIGHT

- Hours of daylight in Providence on December 21 (shortest day of the year): 9:06
- Hours of daylight in Providence on June 21 (longest day of the year): 15:20
- Hours of daylight in Providence on September 21 and March 21 (equinox): 12:14

Source: New England Weather, New England Climate (University Press of New England, 2003).

NOR'EASTERS

Nor'easters typically occur between October and April and bring with them strong winds and sometimes heavy rain or snow. Nor'easters are caused by severe low pressure systems forming in the Gulf of Mexico or the Atlantic and moving up the East Coast into New England. If the storm is to the west of coastal New England, the result is usually heavy rain, but if the storm is wet and cold enough and moving over the Atlantic, major snowfalls can result. The name nor'easter comes from the counterclockwise air movement of the storm which produces intense northeasterly winds in coastal areas.

A PERFECT STORM, AN IMPERFECT RESPONSE

The December 13, 2007 snowstorm doesn't look overwhelming by the numbers: 6.2 inches of snow fell, a substantial amount, but a mere dusting compared to the Blizzard of '78, or the January 2005 storm which left behind 23 inches of the white stuff in Providence. What was notable was the inadequate and wrongheaded response to the storm.

The flakes began to come down steadily in late morning, and schools, government offices and businesses responded by sending people home. By early afternoon, snow was falling heavily and there was gridlock in and around Providence as everyone simultaneously tried to get out of town. The crush of traffic trying to negotiate I-95 and other roads prevented plows from getting through, and long after the snow had tapered off, highways remained clogged and cars, trucks and school buses were stranded. Twenty-minute commutes turned into six-hour nightmares, and some people simply abandoned their vehicles. Well after dark, and even as late as 10 pm, there were Providence school buses with children on board still stuck on the roads.

In the storm's aftermath, fingers pointed everywhere - at Governor Don Carcieri (who was visiting troops in Iraq), at the Providence Schools Superintendent, and at the Providence and Rhode Island Emergency Management Agencies (EMA). The EMA Directors were ultimately fired, and other officials' reputations took a hit as well.

IT'S NOT THE HEAT, IT'S THE HUMIDITY

Like much of the northeastern US, Rhode Island is humid and it can feel pretty darn sticky in the summer. Statistically, however, it's not much more humid in summer than other times of year — it's just that when

TAKE 5 TONY PETRARCA'S TOP FIVE
FORECASTING CHALLENGES

Tony Petrarca is Chief Meteorologist at WPRI Channel 12 and has been forecasting weather in southern New England since 1987. A graduate of Vermont's Lyndon State College, Petrarca was born and raised in Warwick and attended Toll Gate High School. He has been voted "Most Accurate Meteorologist" numerous times in the *Rhode Island Monthly* annual reader's poll, has received multiple Associated Press Awards for "Best Weathercast," and has many nominations for New England Emmy awards. Tony frequently visits local elementary schools to teach kids about the weather, and serves on the Board of the Rhode Island chapter of the Multiple Sclerosis Society. He lives in West Warwick with his wife and two children.

1. **The rain/snow line**. Forecasting the rain/snow divide through the smallest state in the country is surprisingly tough. We've had winter storms where the far northwest corner of the state gets 14 inches of snow, while the coastline picks up little or none. Subtle rises in elevation and being surrounded by mild ocean currents can play havoc on predicting precipitation type.

2. **Hurricane track and intensity**. Well, to be fair, this is challenging for all areas from Maine to Florida. What is unique to Rhode Island and southern New England is that at our latitude, a hurricane's forward speed is accelerating. This means we don't have the luxury of extra time to evacuate coastal residents. A slower approach would give us more time to react. The Hurricane of 1938 had an approach speed of almost 60 mph! Also, because waters here are cooler than the tropics, storms normally weaken as they approach — to what extent that weakening occurs is a forecaster's dilemma.

the mercury hits 90, a high humidity reading is very noticeable. August, September and October are the most humid months in Rhode Island, and the air is driest in January and February. Like most places, humidity readings are usually higher in the morning than the afternoon.

Source: Northeast Regional Climate Center.

3. **Snow accumulation amounts** (see item #1). Ocean waters have a huge influence on temperatures in the lowest levels of the atmosphere. Our winter storms can bring a wide variety of precipitation — rain, freezing rain, sleet, wet snow, and dry snow. It is easier to make snow accumulation forecasts with storms that begin and end as snow, but throw in all that other junk and you have a hard time.

4. **Thunderstorm intensity**. Most of our strong to severe thunderstorms occur away from the coast, especially north and west of Providence. Why? Well, these storms love hot temperatures, but as severe storms head south and east from the Berkshires of Massachusetts, they sometimes run into a cool marine air layer off the ocean and weaken very rapidly. It's tricky to predict whether the cool air off the ocean will penetrate far enough inland to weaken an otherwise violent thunderstorm. To make matters even more complicated, sometimes local sea breezes will create showers and thunder. Just another example of how the ocean plays a huge role in local weather.

5. **The Back Door Cold Front**. Boy, these can be tricky too. It's a nickname we give to a cold front that sneaks in from the northeast off the Atlantic. Most of our cold fronts approach from the west or northwest. Backdoors usually occur in late spring and it's like night and day depending which side of the front you are on -- one side can have drizzle and chilly temps, while the other is bright and warm. Often, as the "Back Door" sneaks in, temps can drop 25 degrees in one hour. I say "sneak in," because sometimes our computer models have a difficult time predicting how the front will move. Bottom line, the day could turn out sunny and 60 degrees, or damp and 38 degrees.

ON A CLEAR DAY, YOU CAN SEE . . . PAWTUCKET

Clear skies in Rhode Island are distributed more or less evenly throughout the year.

- Clear days per year: 98
- Partly cloudy days per year: 103

The Blizzard of '78

The Blizzard of '78 remains the touchstone weather event for Rhode Islanders, and the much joked about tendency of Ocean Staters to rush out and stock up on bread and milk at the sign of a few winter flakes is a legacy of that famous late 70s nor'easter.

The storm began on the morning of February 6, 1978 and ended the evening of the following day. Once the snow began falling, it took only a few hours for high winds to produce major drifts, paralyzing the capital city such that even snowmobiles had difficulty negotiating the roads. T.F. Green airport closed, as did schools, government offices and most businesses. With the major arteries out of Providence impassable and littered with abandoned cars, many people were stranded in the city and were forced to take refuge in churches, hospitals and even the downtown Outlet Department Store. Throughout the state, offices, factories and anywhere with a roof and walls became impromptu shelters, whether officially so designated or not.

Governor Joseph Garrahy hunkered down in the State House, and his red plaid shirt became the sartorial motif of the disaster. In order to enable the National Guard to provide emergency services and clear the streets, Providence was effectively quarantined and travel into the city prohibited. Mayor Buddy Cianci even imposed a curfew on pedestrians. Army National Guard helicopters at Quonset Point were used to ferry critically ill people to hospitals, and crews worked round the clock so that T.F. Green Airport could be cleared to allow Army engineers to arrive from Georgia with equipment to aid in snow removal. The response to the storm resulted in testy exchanges between Providence Mayor Cianci, a Republican, and Democratic Governor Garrahy, whom

- Cloudy days per year: 164
- Clearest month: October (11 clear days on average)
- Cloudiest month: May (6 clear days, 10 partly cloudy days, 15 cloudy days)

Readings taken at T.F. Green Airport.

Source: cityrating.com.

Cianci thought was short shifting Providence, while at the same time grabbing credit for obtaining federal aid for the state.

The storm was a full-fledged disaster, but there were bright spots. As often happens in times of crisis, many people rose to the occasion, helping neighbors and often total strangers survive the ordeal. It was also a bonanza for kids (and many grownups), who received a week's vacation in a winter wonderland with unlimited opportunities for sledding, fort building and snowball throwing. And, amazingly, several days after the big snow, while Providence effectively remained shut down, several thousand fans skied, snowshoed and walked to the Civic Center to watch the Providence College Friars basketball team do battle with the visiting North Carolina Tarheels.

BLIZZARD FACTS:
- National Weather Service official snowfall: 28.6 in. (T.F. Green Airport)
- Deepest National Weather Service unofficial snowfall: 54 in. (Woonsocket)
- Number of abandoned cars towed from highways and streets in and around Providence: approximately 5,000
- Trips made by the National Guard to transport medicine and medical personnel: 3,527
- Number of motorists rescued by the RI National Guard 2,968 (1,000 motorists spent the first night in their cars)
- Number of people sheltered: 9,150 (66 shelters)
- Number of deaths attributed to the blizzard: 21

HURRICANES

Survivors of the Great Hurricane of 1938 and 1954's Hurricane Gloria can attest to Rhode Island's susceptibility to severe maritime storms.

The September 21, 1938 hurricane came almost without warning, and had a devastating effect upon the state. It ranks as Rhode Island's worst natural disaster and killed 262 people, with the Westerly area particularly hard hit. When it came ashore, the hurricane was rated a category three storm and had sustained wind speeds of over 120 mph, downing trees and power lines, uprooting non-permanent structures and smashing windows.

The high winds were serious, but the real damage was caused by sea surges which created waves as high as 30 feet, some of which permanently altered parts of southern Rhode Island's shore. Up and down coastal Rhode Island, there was substantial damage as roads, piers, houses, restaurants and warehouses simply washed into the sea. There was major destruction inland as well, with numerous collapsed barns and hundreds of thousands of felled trees in the western part of the state.

Rhode Island's urban areas weren't spared either, as 12 to 14 foot storm surges came up through Narragansett Bay and flooded downtown Providence. Cars were submerged, and people were forced to the upper floors and fire escapes of buildings to beat the water, which rose to seven feet above ground level. The streets became rat infested canals of filthy water, and water filled the Biltmore Hotel and the city's office buildings.

Sixteen years later, Rhode Island was struck once more. Hurricane Carol, also poorly forecast, hit on August 31, 1954, again blasting the Ocean State with high winds and storm surges. Carol was not as devastating as the 1938 hurricane, although it caused major damage and killed 19 people. Downtown Providence flooded nearly as badly as in 1938, causing thousands of cars to be declared total losses, and destroying many businesses.

In order to protect Providence from future storms, the Fox Point Hurricane Barrier was constructed. The barrier was completed in 1966, and consists of a series of gates, dykes and a pumping station. It is credited with

They said it

"We all went to Rocky Point. Everything was wrecked. The Ferris wheel, the roller coasters, and all that was flattened. . . . The big shore dinner hall was wrecked, and that big pier they had there was gone. The arcade was flattened and we found pennies, whole pocketfuls. Pennies everywhere. Went home rich that day."

– 14 year-old Bernard Cournoyer describing the day after the 1938 Hurricane. From the Rhode Island Historical Society Archives, quoted in the *Providence Journal*.

saving the city from major flooding when Hurricane Bob struck in 1991.

Hurricanes are a notable part of the state's history, and major past storms include an 1869 wallop, as well as the Great Gale of 1815 which has been compared in intensity to the hurricane of 1938.

DAR SHE BLOWS

Spring is the windiest time of the year in the Ocean State with March and April boasting average wind speeds of 11.9 mph in Providence. The least windy month is August, with an average wind speed of 9.2 mph. Providence's yearly average wind speed is 10.4 mph, which makes it less windy than Boston (12.4 mph average) and Bridgeport, CT (11.7 mph), but windier than Hartford, CT (8.4 mph), Worcester, MA (10.1 mph), Concord, NH (6.7 mph), Burlington, VT (9.0 mph) and Portland, ME (8.7 mph).

Source: Northeast Regional Climate Center.

Did you know. . .

that the most severe winter weather event in Rhode Island history may have been the "Great Snow of 1717"? Drifts of ten to twenty feet made travel between colony villages, and even houses, near impossible.

SMOG GETS IN YOUR EYES

Providence might not be Cairo, but like much of the northeastern US, Rhode Island does have elevated ozone levels. Environmental Protection Agency (EPA) monitors in Kent, Washington and Providence counties record ozone levels that average .082 parts per million, which is out of

TAKE5 JOHN GHIORSE'S FIVE MOST
MEMORABLE RHODE ISLAND WEATHER EVENTS
OF THE PAST 40 YEARS

Warwick resident John Ghiorse retired in 2009 as a meteorologist on behalf of WJAR Channel 10. Ghiorse began his career in broadcast meteorology in 1966, following four years as a weather officer with the US Air Force. Ghiorse was one of the first television weathercasters with actual training in meteorology, having studied at Penn State, as well as earning an undergraduate chemistry degree at Harvard.

In 2007, Ghiorse was inducted into the Silver Circle of the New England Chapter of the National Academy of Television Arts and Sciences, which recognizes distinguished service of more than 25 years to the television industry. Rhode Islanders are well familiar with the "Ghiorse Factor," a shorthand measure Ghiorse devised in the 1970s to indicate how pleasant it is to be outside: "10" represents a glorious day, and "0" absolutely miserable conditions.

1. **The Blizzard of '78 (February 6, 7, 8, 1978)**. Without doubt, Numero Uno. It dumped three to four feet of snow in two days, and literally closed Providence for a week. Every Rhode Islander has a story (or two, or three!). Mine started on Monday, February 6. While doing weather broadcasts all day and night, I catnapped on the floor of the Weather Center. Nights two and three: I bedded down in the furniture department of the Outlet Department Store (the TV studio was located on its 5th floor). Night four: I snowshoed to the Holiday Inn. Day five: I got home on a snowmobile for a shower, and then snowmobiled back to work for the six p.m. news.

compliance with the EPA's standard eight-hour average of .075 parts per million. Rhode Island's air quality is comparable to that of Hartford, CT, the Boston area and Cape Cod, but is substantially worse than what prevails in Vermont and most of New Hampshire and Maine.

Source: Environmental Protection Agency.

2. **Hurricane Bob (August 19, 1991)**. The storm caused extensive damage from the East Bay to Cape Cod and the Islands. Lucky me, I was on a cruise ship headed to Bermuda. Unlucky me, the ship went through Bob's eye before it hit New England. There was heavy damage on the ship but we made it, and the weather for the sail back home was perfect!

3. **All Time Record Snow Season (December 1995 - April 1996)**. By February 15, 1996 we had a season total of 78 inches, breaking the previous record set in 1947-'48. Then it rained and thawed. All the mounds of snow melted. But there was more, much more, to come. It began snowing again on March 2, followed by several more storms, the last of which occurred on April 10. The season's final total: 106.1 inches, smashing the old record by nearly 2 ½ feet!

4. **All Time Record High Temperature (104 degrees, August 2, 1975)**. My tennis doubles partner and I played in the finals of a local tournament that afternoon. We weren't so hot … we lost to a couple of teenagers. We also lost about 10 pounds apiece, which we regained quickly gulping our beverage of choice. It also helped soothe our bruised egos.

5. **Christmas Day 1980**. Santa and his reindeer felt right at home in Rhode Island. The temperature was 35 at midnight, but plunged to 3 above by daybreak and, in spite of bright sun, remained at zero from 9 a.m. to 5 p.m., then dove to 10 below zero that night. With winds gusting at 30-50 mph, the wind chill was 25 to 45 below.

They said it

CLIMATE CHANGE

There is substantial evidence that Rhode Island is getting warmer. Rhode Island's mean annual temperature increased 2.3° F between 1895 and 2000, the greatest increase among the six New England states. Other evidence of a warming trend includes rising sea levels (Newport has increased 10 inches and Providence 7.5 inches in the last 100 years) and a 3° F increase in the temperature of Narragansett Bay.

As Rhode Island gets warmer it is also getting wetter — precipitation is up, although snowfall has declined. Of concern is that as Rhode Island continues to heat up, further increases in precipitation will occur, causing coastal areas to flood more frequently, as well as substantial beach erosion. In addition to affecting the state's flora and fauna, warming is also expected to have an impact on the agriculture and tourism industries, and will produce a rise in heat-related deaths and asthma.

Did you know...

that the Juliett 484, a vintage Soviet sub moored at Collier Point Park near the Port of Providence, sank as result of heavy rain in April 2007? The sub, which had been open to the public as the floating Russian Sub Museum, succumbed following a powerful nor'easter which grounded its hull.

TAKE 5 AVERAGE DAYS PER YEAR WITH PRECIPITATION FOR FIVE AMERICAN CITIES

1. San Diego, CA	42
2. Denver, CO	89
3. Washington, DC	118
4. **Providence**	**125**
5. Portland, OR	152

Source: Northeast Regional Climate Center.

GROWING SEASON

Rhode Island's growing season averages five to six months, with considerable variation within the state. The southern coastal areas have substantially longer growing seasons than inland locales. For Kingston, the growing season is typically May 8 to October 3, or 147 days. For Newport, 200 days is average, and for Warwick 188 days.

Source: Northeast Regional Climate Center.

Did you know. . .

that there is a 37 percent chance of having a white Christmas in Providence? A white Christmas is defined as having a minimum of an inch of snow on the ground on December 25.

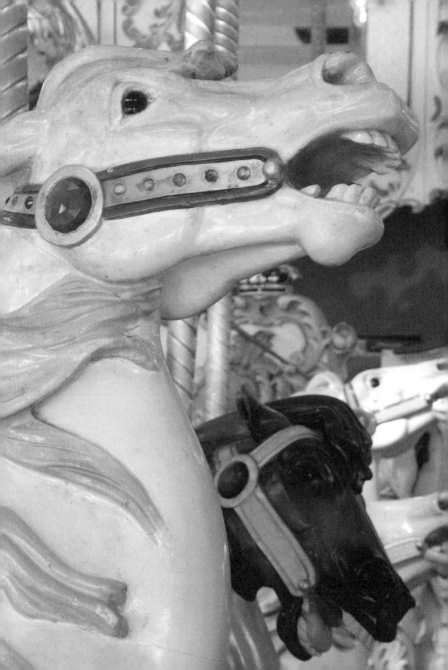

Culture

Rhode Island has long been an important literary and artistic center, and it boasts one of the highest populations of artists per capita in the country. The state is also widely known for the applied arts, the long-standing jewelry industry embodying the intertwining of design, craft and production.

In recent years, some of the state's vacant industrial spaces have found new life as artists' studios and lofts, and arts and culture have revitalized areas of Providence and Pawtucket.

Popular culture and entertainment are also important in Rhode Island. Not only are Rhode Islanders avid sports fans and movie buffs, the state has proven itself a wellspring of talented athletes and actors.

THE ENVELOPE, PLEASE

Two Rhode Islanders received 2008 Oscar nominations. Richard Jenkins was nominated in the Best Actor category for his portrayal of an emotionally distant professor who becomes enmeshed in the lives of two undocumented immigrants in *The Visitor*, while Viola Davis received a Best Supporting Actress nomination for playing the mother of a boy who may have been sexually abused by a priest in *Doubt*.

The Illinois-born Jenkins came to Rhode Island in 1970 and lives in Cumberland. He has been appearing in films for over thirty years, and former Cumberlandites Peter and Bobby Farrelly have used him in a number of their movies. Of late, Jenkins has assumed a higher screen profile, playing the dead patriarch Nathaniel Fisher in the HBO series *Six Feet Under*, and appearing as a fitness club manager in the Coen brothers' *Burn After Reading* and the father in the Will Ferrell comedy *Step Brothers*. Jenkins used to be an actor at Trinity Repertory Company in Providence, and also served as its Artistic Director for several years.

Viola Davis was born in 1965 in South Carolina, but as an infant moved to Central Falls where her family was among the few African Americans. Davis's father was a horse groomer at Lincoln Downs and Narragansett Park, and the family was poor, living in rat-infested buildings. The Central Falls High School grad studied at Rhode Island College and New York's Juilliard School, and now lives in Los Angeles.

Davis has appeared in a number of movies including *Madea Goes to Jail*, *Solaris*, and *Antwone Fisher*, and her television credits include *Law & Order: Special Victims Unit*, *Traveler* and *City of Angels*. Davis also has extensive stage experience, acting in several Trinity Rep productions, as well as receiving a Tony award for her performance in the August Wilson play *King Hedley II*.

FAMILY GUY

It's a typical suburban Rhode Island family: overweight doofus dad, exasperated wife, beefy dimwit son, and homely daughter. Rounding out the animated Griffin clan, who live in the fictional Quahog, Rhode Island (allegedly Cranston, but seemingly a pastiche of Rhode Island towns) is a diabolical infant genius who speaks with a British accent, and a talking dog who also drinks and smokes. In the tradition of *The Simpsons*, the highly self-conscious and self-referential *Family Guy* often riffs on Broadway musicals, and features numerous cut-away vignettes and non-plot related one-off gags. The Fox Television series is packed with real and pseudo Rhode Island references, among the more obvious ones are the Providence skyline, Buddy Cianci Jr. High School, Brown

University and Happy-Go-Lucky Toys (a stand in for Hasbro).

RISD grad Seth MacFarlane created *Family Guy*, and voices the characters of Griffin paterfamilias Peter, infant Stewie and dog, Brian. MacFarlane also developed the animated series *American Dad*, and is a truly lucky man. On the morning of September 11, 2001 MacFarlane, who had delivered a speech at RISD the day previous, was to have flown from Boston to Los Angeles. He missed his flight, and the plane he failed to catch hit the World Trade Center.

I WILL SURVIVE

For reasons not altogether clear, Rhode Islanders were proportionately overrepresented in the early days of the *Survivor* television show.

- **Richard Hatch** of Middletown was the winner in 2000, the program's inaugural season. The eccentric Hatch, a corporate trainer and openly gay man not afraid to stride about in the buff, netted a million dollars from his reality show victory. He then parlayed his celebrity status and curious mix of charisma and obnoxiousness into a talk radio gig on a Boston station. Unfortunately, he neglected to pay Uncle Sam his due on his newfound wealth and was sent to prison in 2006 for tax evasion.
- **Elizabeth Filarski Hasselback** grew up in Cranston and appeared on *Survivor: The Australian Outback* in 2001. She is married to sportscaster and former NFL quarterback Tim Hasselback, and is a co-host on the NBC talk show *The View*. Since joining the show in 2003, Hasselback's outspoken conservative views have caused her to butt heads with her co-hosts, as well as several guests. Coincidentally, another Rhode Islander, East Providence native Meredith Vieira, was also a member of *The View* team before leaving to co-anchor *The Today Show*.
- **Helen Glover** of Portsmouth made it to the final four of *Survivor: Thailand* in 2002. The athletic Glover is a former US Navy water survival instructor, and currently hosts a talk show on Providence radio station 920 WHJJ.

The Farrelly brothers

Need a Rhode Island travelogue? No better way to get it than to digest the Rhode Island-raised Farrelly brothers oeuvre, notably *Dumb & Dumber* (1994), *There's Something About Mary* (1998) and *Me, Myself and Irene* (2000), three physical comedies written, directed and produced by the brothers, and filmed at least in part in the Ocean State.

Peter (1956-) and Bobby (1958-) were also behind the 1999 film *Outside Providence*, which is set in their home state. The screenplay was adapted from Peter's 1988 novel, and was directed by fellow Rhode Islander Michael Corrente. In the Farrelly films, everywhere from Providence's Kennedy Plaza to Main Street in Jamestown and the Mount St. Charles Academy hockey arena in Woonsocket gets a look, as do such landmarks as the Big Blue Bug. And, in *Me, Myself and Irene*, Jim Carrey sports a Rhode Island State Trooper uniform.

The Farrellys, who got their start in the entertainment business in 1992 when they penned a Seinfeld episode, grew up in Cumberland with their three sisters, doctor father and nurse mother. They entered the movie business in an indirect fashion. Younger brother Bobby, flush with an undergraduate geology degree, had moved to Los Angeles to market a round beach towel, a concept he and a friend had invented, but which ultimately led nowhere. Brother Peter, a Providence College grad, was already in L.A., having moved there to write after completing an MFA in creative writing at Columbia University. Peter asked Bobby to give him some input on his work, and soon the brothers were collaborating.

The rest is history. Their breakthrough effort, *Dumb & Dumber*, wound up grossing several hundred million dollars and put them on the map as filmmakers. Since then, the Farrellys have produced a number of comedies, including *The Heartbreak Kid*, *Fever Pitch*, *Shallow Hal* and *Kingpin*.

FOLK AND JAZZ IN NEWPORT

The Newport Jazz Festival was founded in 1954 by George Wein, who five years later started the Newport Folk Festival. The music is front and center, but the city of Newport's stunning ocean vistas and historic buildings are an important part of the mix.

The Jazz Festival's first season featured Ella Fitzgerald, Dizzy Gillespie and Billie Holiday, and since then Newport has remained a premier event, attracting leading jazz, blues and R&B performers. In the 2000s, veterans Aretha Franklin, Sonny Rollins, and Dave Brubeck made appearances, as did a new generation of musicians. There have also been tributes to jazz masters, and an increased focus

TAKE 5 FIVE RHODE ISLAND
FEATURE LENGTH DOCUMENTARIES

1. **Buddy** (2005; 90 mins). Directed by Cherry Arnold and narrated by James Woods. *Buddy* charts the rise and fall, and rise and fall, of Vincent "Buddy" Cianci as Providence mayor.

2. **Italian Americans and Federal Hill** (2006; 89 mins). Directed by Jon Raben. *Italian Americans* lovingly documents Rhode Island's Little Italy in the era of push-carts, corner markets and an all powerful Catholic Church.

3. **You Must Be This Tall** (2007; 81 mins). Directed by David Bettencourt. *You Must Be This Tall* is a nostalgic look at the now demolished Rocky Point Amusement Park in Warwick.

4. **Traces of the Trade: A Story from the Deep North** (2008; 86 mins). Directed by Katrina Browne. *Traces of the Trade* shows the contemporary members of the DeWolf family, including the filmmaker herself, grappling with their family's past as prominent Rhode Island slave traders.

5. **Accelerating America** (2008; 90 mins). Directed by Timothy Hotchner. *Accelerating America* is about an innovative Providence high school helmed by a quadriplegic principal dedicated to giving drop-outs a second chance.

on international music.

The Newport Folk Festival debuted in 1959 and has a similarly storied past, attracting top folkies including Joan Baez, Joni Mitchell, Peter, Paul and Mary, Willie Nelson, Janis Joplin, and Pete Seeger (one of the festival's founders).

In 1965, history was made when a scruffy 24-year-old took the stage and plugged in his guitar. Bob Dylan had gone electric. The legend is that Dylan was booed off the Newport stage for his electric affront to folk sensibilities; however, some contend that the crowd was in fact yelling, frustrated with the brevity and poor sound quality of Dylan's set. Regardless, the incident remains an integral part of rock mythology.

The current version of the festival mixes old timers with new

TAKE5 FIVE HOLLYWOOD MOVIES FILMED IN RHODE ISLAND

1. *The Great Gatsby* (1974) with Robert Redford and Mia Farrow. Francis Ford Coppola's screenplay was based on the F. Scott Fitzgerald classic. Rhode Island locations include Newport and Bristol.

2. *Amistad* (1997) with Morgan Freeman, Nigel Hawthorne and Anthony Hopkins. Directed by Steven Speilberg. Rhode Island locations include Newport, Pawtucket and Providence.

3. *Meet Joe Black* (1998) with Brad Pitt and Anthony Hopkins. The Rhode Island location was the Aldrich Mansion in Warwick.

4. *Underdog* (2007) with James Belushi, and *Hachiko* (2009) with Richard Gere. Underdog was principally shot in Providence, including scenes at the Rhode Island State House. *Hachiko*, also with a canine in a lead role, was filmed in Bristol and Woonsocket, and at the University of Rhode Island and Providence's Columbus Theatre.

5. *27 Dresses* (2008) with Katherine Heigl. Rhode Island locations include Cumberland, Providence and Goddard Memorial State Park.

names, and festival producers are defining folk increasingly broadly. Acts who have taken the stage at Fort Adams State Park in recent years have included such non-folkies as Jimmy Buffet, rock bands the Black Crowes and Calexico, and Dylan's son, Jakob Dylan.

ART

Rhode Island is home to numerous art galleries, and Providence sponsors a monthly Gallery Night. Providence's neighbor to the north, Pawtucket, has also become a hot spot for the arts in the last decade, and a number of its mill spaces have been converted to artists' studios. South County is similarly rich in artists and artisans of various stripes. The Wickford Art Festival, held in Wickford Village near North Kingstown every July, attracts approximately 75,000 visitors annually. The two-day festival began in 1962, and exhibits original work by about 250 artists.

Among Rhode Island's more prominent museums are the Newport Art Museum, which is housed in the 1862 Griswold House (a National Historic Landmark), and the Rhode Island School of Design (RISD) Museum. The RISD Museum possesses an impressive and diverse collection, and opened its new Chace Center in 2008. The contemporary structure is attached to the older labyrinth-like Benefit Street building, and the two contain over 80,000 works of art. The collection includes sculptures from ancient Greece, Rome, and Egypt; centuries-old Asian artifacts; French Impressionist paintings by the likes of Monet, Cezanne, Rodin and Matisse; and works from American masters including Homer, Sargent and Cassat. In addition to paintings and sculptures, RISD's collection also includes textiles, furniture, decorative art objects, costumes, drawings, contemporary art and photography.

RISD the school was founded in 1877, and is one of the country's leading art and design institutions. The school's 2,200 undergraduate and graduate students choose from among sixteen majors including painting, digital media, architecture, film, glass, industrial design and jewelry/metalsmithing. A number of RISD grads are active as artists and teachers in the state.

TAKE 5 LARRY (AND BUSTER) BONOFF'S
TOP FIVE WARWICK MUSICAL THEATER ACTS

Larry Bonoff is a fourth generation music promoter whose father, Buster Bonoff, founded the Warwick Musical Theater (known as the "the Tent") on Route 2 in Warwick in 1955. In the 1950s and 60s, the Warwick Musical Theater (WMT) played host to numerous touring productions of Broadway musicals, and in the 1970s was a popular venue for Las Vegas style performers. Throughout the 1980s and 90s, top comedians, rock bands, country and western acts, and even professional wrestlers took the WMT stage. The WMT closed in 1999, but Larry Bonoff keeps the flame alive as head of the Bonoff Foundation, which is dedicated to preserving and displaying the records of multiple generations of entertainment promoters on both sides of his family.

1. **Jack Benny**. One of the great get-on-stage-and-entertain-you guys. I was a kid at the time he played the Tent and a fan of his TV show. My family went to dinner with Jack at the Great House restaurant, and I couldn't believe it when he picked up the tab — on TV he was always so cheap! That's when I learned that people in show business aren't the same in real life as they are on stage.

2. **Liberace**. The greatest showman and the greatest human. He enjoyed life and he enjoyed people, and had an incredible memory for names and faces. After performing for two hours he'd set up a table and do an autograph session. "Every person I sign for tonight will be a fan for life," he told me.

3. **Mel Tillis**. I knew Mel from Arizona and stayed at his house in Tennessee a number of times. My father promoted shows at the Phoenix Star Theatre (now named the Celebrity Theatre) starting in 1964, and I got a real taste of country music by spending all my winters out West — this was before country was really accepted in the

Northeast. Mel was the first winner of the Country Music Association's Comedian of the Year award, and is a member of the Country Music Hall of Fame. Along with Eddy Arnold, he was one of the first country acts to play in Rhode Island.

4. **Vince Gill, Alabama, Reba McEntire, Brooks & Dunn** (Combination). I was the first promoter to book a lot of big name, big dollar country acts in the Northeast. In the 1980s, these artists took country from the Urban Cowboy stereotype to network TV and Vegas type show rooms. They had great tunes which kept alive the classic American cowboy themes, while also becoming the family-oriented songs of that era.

5. **Johnny Carson**. He did five shows in three days in 1978 as a favor to my father. It was extremely rare for Carson to do stand-up gigs, and he was great. He had a real Nebraska humbleness to him — all he asked for backstage was a hamburger and a Coke.

HONORABLE MENTIONS: **Bill Cosby** — I once shared a helicopter ride with him as he traveled between back-to-back shows in Arizona and found him to be an incredible person in terms of how much he cared about the world. **Jay Leno** — a gifted comedian, but talent only goes so far — a really great guy.

BUSTER BONOFF'S TOP 5 (Dad passed away in 2000, but I think he would approve): 1. **Liberace**, 2. **Sammy Davis Jr.** 3. **Nat King Cole** 4. **Vince Gill** 5. **George Burns**.

HONORABLE MENTIONS: **The Mills Brothers**, **Harry Chapin**, **Don Rickles**.

H.P. Lovecraft

H.P. Lovecraft (1890-1937) is considered a pioneer of the modern horror genre. He invested his often supernatural stories with a powerful mystical foreboding and gloom, and explored the horror that lies within the human mind and soul. In Lovecraft's work, forces from the sea, other worlds and beyond the grave invariably intrude on everyday life. "Reality" can never be trusted.

Lovecraft was born in Providence and lived most of his life on the city's East Side, with a 1920s interlude of several years when he was married to a Russian woman and lived in Brooklyn. The marriage ended in divorce, and Lovecraft returned home to Providence. A depressive and mentally fragile polymath whose interests ranged from astronomy to mythology, Lovecraft suffered a breakdown before graduating high school and never earned his diploma. Instead, he spent several years isolated at home with his mother, writing. Lovecraft's childhood was difficult; his father (who spent five years in a coma when H.P. was young) died when Lovecraft was eight. Moreover, H.P.'s mother, who was psychologically cruel to her son, suffered from mental illness and was eventually hospitalized.

H.P. (the initials stand for Howard Philip) Lovecraft was a prolific essayist, poet, writer of pulp fiction and correspondent. He wrote tens of thousands of letters in his lifetime. A keen intellect who self-published much of his writing, Lovecraft was a proto-blogger forever churning out one thing or another drawing on his immense store of knowledge and his experiences traveling about the eastern US and Canada. He died of intestinal cancer in 1937.

Lovecraft was deeply attached to Providence's East Side, its College Hill neighborhood in particular. Prospect Terrace Park overlooking downtown was a favorite spot, as was Benefit Street. He wrote numerous stories and essays about the various houses he lived in, visited and passed by in his promenades about the area. Lovecraft is buried in Swan Point Cemetery on Blackstone Boulevard, and fans gather for a yearly memorial service at one of his favorite haunts, the Ladd Observatory, at Hope and Doyle Streets. There are also occasional Lovecraft walking tours of the East Side, and the great man of horror's papers are housed at the John Hay Library at Brown University.

HAVING FUN ISN'T HARD, WHEN YOU'VE GOT A LIBRARY CARD

Rhode Island is home to two of North America's most venerable institutions of the printed word: Newport's Redwood Library and Athenaeum, and the Providence Athenaeum.

The Redwood opened in 1750, and it is the country's oldest surviving lending library, as well as the oldest library building in continuous use in the US. The library's Grecian inspired building on Bellevue Avenue is a gem, and has served as home away from home for some of America's brightest cultural lights including Edith Wharton, Henry Wadsworth Longfellow, Gilbert Stuart, and Henry James.

The Redwood is still very much a going concern, and boasts 160,000 volumes, up from the 751 books present in the founding collection. Redwood is open to the general population, but precedes the era of the free library; subscribers pay a yearly fee, while proprietors own shares and pay a yearly assessment.

The Providence Athenaeum has a similarly august history, having been founded in 1753. It is housed in a 1838 Greek Revival building on Benefit Street, and was frequented by H.P. Lovecraft, as well as by Edgar Allan Poe during the latter's time in Providence in the 1840s. Like its Newport counterpart, the Providence Athenaeum is a subscription library, although like Newport it also sponsors activities and events that are free and open to the general public.

In addition to these two classic jewels, there are hundreds of public libraries in the state; the Ocean State Libraries network includes 50 library systems and access to a combined 4.5 million items.

Did you know. . .

that John Updike's 1984 novel *The Witches of Eastwick*, as well as its 2008 follow up *The Widows of Eastwick*, is set in fictional Eastwick, Rhode Island, a crossbreeding of East Greenwich and Wickford?

Not Just for Kids: David Macaulay and Chris Van Allsburg

David Macaulay, the man behind *The Way Things Work* and other books, earned an architecture degree at RISD in 1969. He never practiced in the field, but has used his skills to create a series of deftly illustrated volumes describing and explaining various types of buildings and structures. His debut effort was *Cathedral* in 1973, and he has followed that up with a raft of titles including *Pyramid, Castle, Mill* and *Mosque*. Macaulay has also written and illustrated more fanciful picture books, including *Black and White*, *Baa*, and *Angelo*.

Macaulay's best known book is the New York Times' bestseller *The Way Things Work*, which was revised in 1998 as *The New Way Things Work*. In 2006, Macaulay received a half-million-dollar MacArthur Fellowship (sometimes known as a genius grant) in recognition of his work. His latest book, *The Way We Work* (2008), was years in the making and uses clever illustrations to depict the ultimate machine — the human body. Macaulay, for many years an East Side of Providence resident and RISD teacher, currently lives in Vermont.

Another East Sider, Michigan-born Chris Van Allsburg, received his MFA from RISD in 1975. He was working as a sculptor when David Macaulay saw some illustrations he had done and suggested that Van Allsburg try his hand at children's books. Van Allsburg's first book, *The Garden of Abdul Gasazi*, was published in 1979 and since then he has produced 15 more including *The Polar Express*, *Jumanji*, *The Mysteries of Harris Burdick*, *Two Bad Ants*, and *Probuditi*. Van Allsburg's richly detailed illustrations and mysterious fable-like stories often leave the reader guessing where reality leaves off and fantasy begins. Several of his books have been made into Hollywood movies, and Van Allsburg has won numerous awards for his writing and illustrating.

They said it

"I am Providence."

– Providence horror and supernatural writer
H.P. Lovecraft (1890-1937).

MATILDA SISSIERETTA JOYNER JONES

Matilda Sissieretta Joyner Jones (1869-1933) grew up in Providence and was one of the top entertainers of the late 1800s and early 1900s. The African American Jones, sometimes called "the Black Patti" after Italian soprano Adelina Patti, sang for President Benjamin Harrison at the White House in 1892, as well as before several other presidents, the Prince of Wales and the German Kaiser.

Jones attended the New England Conservatory of Music in Boston, and was an accomplished operatic and popular singer who commanded as much as $2,000 per performance, the top fee for a Black artist of her era. Jones was limited by the racism of the time, and responded by forming her own 40-person touring troupe of singers, dancers, comedians and other performers. She retired in 1915 to Providence, where she remained for the rest of her life taking care of her sick mother, doing church work, and looking after homeless children. Jones died a pauper in 1933, having lost much of her early money to her ex-husband manager, a heavy drinker who squandered much of the couple's funds.

Did you know. . .

that Edgar Allan Poe lived in Providence in the late 1840s? Poe was in town courting local poet, essayist and universal suffrage advocate Sarah Whitman. The two were conditionally engaged, one of the conditions being that Poe stop drinking, something that he was unable to do. The engagement broken, he returned home to Baltimore where he died shortly thereafter.

EDDIE DOWLING

Eddie Dowling, a prodigious vaudeville and Broadway songwriter, actor, playwright, director and producer was one of 17 children. Born Joseph Nelson Goucher in Woonsocket in 1895, in his youth Dowling would sing Irish and French Canadian tunes for change outside taverns in Woonsocket's Social District. Dowling's many credits include the 1940 Pulitzer Prize winning play *The Time of Your Life*, a William Saroyan drama which he both directed and starred in. He also co-directed and starred in the 1945 Broadway premier of Tennessee Williams's *The Glass Menagerie*, and founded the United Service Organization (USO) Camp Shows, which continue to mount productions for US troops at home and abroad. Dowling died in 1976 in Smithfield, and a section of Route 146 is named in his honor.

THE DUNK

The Dunk, as it is called locally, is home to the Providence College men's basketball team and the Providence Bruins hockey squad. The arena opened in 1972, and was formerly known as the Civic Center before Dunkin' Donuts purchased naming rights in 2001.

Located in downtown Providence, the Dunk seats 12,500 for basketball games, and frequently hosts concerts and other events such as circuses and ice shows. Big names who have played the arena include rockers Pink Floyd, Bruce Springsteen and Metallica, as well as croon-

Did you know...

that the Cowsills, a bubblegum rock band from Newport composed of the six Cowsill siblings and their mother, was the inspiration for the television show *The Partridge Family*? The band had its heyday in the late 1960s when it scored several million selling hits, including "Hair" from the eponymous musical.

er Neil Diamond, rapper 50 Cent and tween queen Miley Cyrus/Hannah Montana. The once utilitarian Dunk was upgraded over a period of several years in the 2000s, and now features luxury suites as well as a new scoreboard and a redesigned lobby and concourses.

TAKE 5 FIVE RHODE ISLAND SCHOOL OF DESIGN ALUMNI

1. **Dale Chihuly** (MFA Ceramics, 1968). A glass blower and designer whose enormous and fanciful creations echo the sea and the natural world, the eye patch wearing Chihuly is considered the foremost glass artist of his era. Chihuly established the glass department at RISD in 1969, and in 2008 the RISD Museum inaugurated its new Chace Center with a showing of his work.

2. **Nicole Miller** (BFA Apparel Design, 1973). New York fashion designer and mogul Miller's creations and licensed merchandise show up in department stores, on run-ways and on the backs of Hollywood celebs.

3. **David Byrne** (did not graduate, attended in early 1970s). Musician Byrne founded the influential band the Talking Heads in the mid 1970s with Tina Weymouth (BFA 1974) and Chris Frantz (BFA 1974). In addition to his output with the Talking Heads, Byrne has a number of solo efforts to his credit, collaborated with Brian Eno on two albums and founded the Luaka Bop record label.

4. **Gus Van Sant** (BFA Film/Animation/Video 1975). Film director Van Sant's credits include *Good Will Hunting, Finding Forrester, To Die For, My Own Private Idaho* and *Drugstore Cowboy*.

5. **Jenny Holzer** (MFA Painting 1977; honorary doctorate 2003). A conceptual artist who makes frequent use of words and phrases in her installations, Holzer represented the US at the 1990 Venice Biennale. Holzer has numerous awards, permanent installations and solo shows to her credit, including one at New York's Guggenheim Museum.

Father of American Portraiture

You likely have a Gilbert Stuart picture in your wallet — Stuart created the George Washington portrait found on the one-dollar bill.

Born to Scottish immigrants in 1755 in Saunderstown, Stuart moved to Newport at age seven. As a teen, Stuart studied with a prominent local Scottish painter, and then traveled to England in 1775 where he apprenticed with the renowned American artist Benjamin West. Stuart became a leading London portraitist, and exhibited a painting at the Royal Academy in 1782 called "The Skater (Portrait of William Grant)" which portrayed its subject on skates. This break from the staid portrait tradition of the time won Stuart wide acclaim.

After nearly two decades in England and Ireland, Stuart returned home in 1793, living in New York, Philadelphia and Washington, DC, before finally settling in Boston in 1805 (he died there in 1828). Stuart would complete over 1,000 portraits in his lifetime; in addition to Washington, he painted Presidents Adams, Jefferson, Madison and Monroe, as well as military heroes and other prominent Americans. Stuart was known as a bon vivant and spendthrift who was often close to financial ruin — his interval in Ireland was a move chosen in order to avoid debtor's prison.

Stuart remains an important artist, but more significantly, he is responsible for establishing the images of Washington and other important Americans of the Federal era in the popular mindset. One of Stuart's Washington portraits hangs in the East Room of the White House, and his paintings are exhibited in leading museums in the US and abroad. Locally, there is a magnificent Washington portrait of Stuart's on display in the Rhode Island State House, and the Gilbert Stuart Birthplace and Museum in Saunderstown features reproductions of his work.

They said it

"We don't have oil — we have culture. That's the asset that's here, so I want to be able to activate that asset. And that can lead to economic prosperity, because we have what's authentic and real here."

**– RISD President John Maeda in a 2008
interview with the *Providence Phoenix*.**

VETERAN'S MEMORIAL AUDITORIUM

Construction on the 1,900-seat Veteran's Memorial Auditorium (VMA) in Providence began in the 1920s, but the venue did not open until 1950. The Depression put a halt to work on the VMA, and it was not until post-WWII that the building was completed. The auditorium was nearly demolished in the 1980s, but was saved and eventually refurbished. The VMA currently hosts Rhode Island Philharmonic concerts and Festival Ballet performances, and is often used by high schools for graduation ceremonies.

The adjacent Masonic Temple building had an even longer gestation period as its construction was halted in 1929, and the partial structure left abandoned until 2004 when building recommenced. The project represented the largest restoration initiative in the history of the state, but in 2007 the Renaissance Providence Hotel, constructed inside the shell of the historic building's once graffiti-scarred façade, opened for business.

Did you know. . .

that actor James Woods, star of the TV show *Shark*, as well as dozens of movies including *Salvador, Nixon, Once Upon a Time in America* and *The Virgin Suicides* grew up in Warwick and attended Pilgrim High School? His younger brother Michael, who died in 2006, was a Democratic mayoral candidate in Warwick in 2000 and 2004.

George M. Cohan: Rhode Island's Yankee Doodle Dandy

If his output had been limited to "Over There," the hugely popular World War I ode which won him a Congressional Medal of Honor, George M. Cohan would still rank among his generation's great songwriters. But Cohan not only captured the spirit of his times in that famous song, he was also incredibly prolific and versatile, excelling as a singer, dancer, actor, director, lyricist and musician.

Cohan was born on July 3, 1878 to a New England Irish Providence family of vaudeville performers; however, throughout his life, in keeping with his trademark patriotic shtick, he claimed to have been born on the fourth of July. Cohan made his performance debut as a violin prodigy, and was soon taking solo turns as a dancer and actor. As a teenager during the 1890s, Cohan barnstormed the country, appearing with his parents and sister under "The Four Cohans" banner.

Cohan was not content to be a hired hand, and while still in his teens was already writing and selling songs and vaudeville bits, demanding to be paid royalties for his creations. Cohan's first Broadway production was *The Governor's Son* in 1901, which he wrote, composed, directed and produced. It was Cohan's position as an impresario, and not just a creative type, that would make him a very wealthy man. Cohan owned theaters, and with his partner Sam H. Harris, produced over 50 plays and revues during a 15-year period in the early twentieth century. As an actor, Cohan bridged the vaudeville and Broadway eras, and was adept in both wisecracking musical roles and serious dramatic efforts.

In addition to "Over There," Cohan also authored other patriotic ditties including "Yankee Doodle Dandy" and "It's a Grand Old Flag." These are probably his greatest legacy, as Cohan had little interest in the burgeoning movie industry, and he predated television. Cohan died in his apartment overlooking Central Park in 1942, and that same year James Cagney played him in a bio-pic.

Did you know. . .

that actor, writer and spoken word performer Spalding Gray was born in 1941 in Providence and grew up in Barrington? A number of Gray's monologues were filmed and made into feature length movies, including *Swimming to Cambodia*, *Monster in a Box* and *Gray's Anatomy*. Gray, brother of *Providence Journal* arts writer Channing Gray, committed suicide in 2004 when he jumped from the Staten Island Ferry.

LUPO'S

Lupo's opened in downtown Providence in 1974, and since then has played host to thousands of performers. It's also sold an awful lot of beer in that time. Brown graduate Rich Lupo has booked everyone from Bo Diddley, James Brown and the Ramones to the Wu-Tang Clan and the Jonas Brothers.

The venue has moved twice, and almost become a casualty of the famed Providence Renaissance. In the 1970s and 80s, when downtown Providence was a near ghost town, Lupo's was a rare bright spot, and the go-to place for music for everyone from suburban metalheads to College Hill dilettantes. As Downcity's fortunes picked up, Lupo's was nearly squeezed out, but has managed to hang on and draw new generations of concert goers. The all-ages six p.m. shows bring in a barely pubescent crowd, in contrast to the graybeards who turn up for rock veterans like Joe Jackson and Ray Davies.

Did you know. . .

that the Rustic Tri-View Theater in North Smithfield, Rhode Island's last remaining drive-in, used to show "adult films" in the 1970s? The drive-in currently operates three screens and shows family friendly fare during the warmer months.

AS220

The non-profit community arts space AS220 describes itself as "part Incubator and part Bazaar." Located in downtown Providence, AS220 is dedicated to showcasing local artists. Shows are not juried, and newcomers rub shoulders with old hands. Its Empire Street location also includes a taqueria and bar, helpful in taking the edge off when the band is not so hot, or the poetry particularly inspiring.

AS220 presents a blizzard of shows, events and exhibitions that include music, visual art, spoken word, poetry, drama, performance art and cabaret, as well as films, lectures and agitprop. AS220 also features residential and work studios for artists, and provides arts programs for at-risk youth. The quality of the programming at AS220 might be uneven, but no one can argue with its diversity (in every sense of the word), or the energy and creativity routinely on display at what has become a local indie-arts landmark.

TAKE 5 TOP FIVE RHODE ISLAND
THEATER BUILDINGS

1. **Providence Performing Arts Center (PPAC), Providence**. Opened in 1928, PPAC cost $2.5 million to build and is a spectacular example of classic 1920s theater design. It was nearly torn down in the 1970s, but escaped demolition and is now listed on the National Register of Historic Places. Substantial renovations and restorations between 1995 and 2005 both returned the theater to its original grandeur, and upgraded it for contemporary audiences. PPAC frequently plays host to the touring versions of Broadway productions, as well as concerts and other spectacles.

2. **Stadium Theatre, Woonsocket**. The Stadium opened in 1926 and is a grand theater in the 1920s movie palace tradition. It fell on hard times in the 1970s when it ceased operations, but was revived in the late 1990s. It now plays host to theatrical productions, concerts and filming for the television series *Brotherhood*.

3. **Jane Pickens Theater and Event Center, Newport**. The building was constructed in 1834, and converted to use as a theater in 1923. In the 1970s it was renamed in honor of singer Jane Pickens (1909-1992), a singer, musician and actress prominent in the 1930s and 40s, and later a Park Avenue and Newport socialite and philanthropist. The theater screens movies, and also hosts concerts, lectures and private parties.

4. **The Granite Theatre, Westerly**. The Granite is a restored Greek Revival Church which was built in 1849. Its steeple was destroyed in the 1938 hurricane. The theater primarily stages classic plays, but also occasionally features cabaret and other performers.

5. **The Gamm Theatre, Pawtucket Armory Annex, Pawtucket**. The armory complex includes a 48,000 square foot Romanesque Revival brick castle, and a 4,500 square foot annex which houses the Sandra Gamm Feinstein Theatre. The complex was completed in 1895 and the annex formerly housed Rhode Island National Guard military vehicles. The space was subsequently a garage for the Pawtucket PD, before being reincarnated as a 137-seat theater.

ANCIENTS AND HORRIBLES

The Ancients and Horribles Parade, held annually on the Fourth of July in Glocester in western Rhode Island, may not have the profile or budget of Bristol's Independence Day extravaganza, but it is the quintessential display of Rhode Island's independent, quirky personality.

TAKE 5 RICK MCGOWAN'S TOP FIVE
RHODE ISLAND ATHLETES
OF THE PAST 40 YEARS

Barrington native Rick McGowan has been covering Rhode Island sports since 1976 on behalf of the *Newport Daily News*.

1. **Ernie DiGregorio**. North Providence HS and Providence College guard, on PC Final Four team in 1973, NBA Rookie of the Year in 1973-74 with the Buffalo Braves. **Top memory:** His three-quarters-of-the-court, behind-the-back pass to Kevin Stacom in the NCAA Final Four in 1973 in St. Louis. *Sports Illustrated* called it one of the greatest moments in Final Four history.

2. **Marvin Barnes**. Central HS in Providence and Providence College forward and center, American Basketball Association (ABA) All-Star with the Spirits of St. Louis, later played for several NBA teams. **Top memory:** Barnes's rebounding and scoring in the 1973 NCAA semifinal game against Memphis State before suffering a knee injury.

3. **Mark van Eeghen**. Cranston West HS, Colgate University, Oakland Raiders and New England Patriots running back. **Top memory:** His play on behalf of the Raiders in the 1981 Super Bowl — Oakland defeated Philadelphia and he was the leading rusher.

4. **Rocco Baldelli**. Bishop Hendricken HS of Warwick volleyball, basketball and baseball player, currently an outfielder for the Red Sox. **Top memory:** First game in the majors. I believe he got a hit.

5. **Brian Lawton**. Mount St. Charles hockey player, first American ever drafted first in the NHL, played professionally with the Minnesota North Stars and several other teams. **Top memory:** One of his games in the 1983 state championship series against Bishop Hendricken, played, I believe, at Brown's Meehan Auditorium.

The parade debuted in 1926, and is a free-form event with no entry fee and no auditions. Participants range from ad-hoc collections of oddballs to Girl Scout troops, war veterans and perennial "Best in Parade" winner Ken Hopkins. There are floats and groups of walkers that defy categorization, as well as "Ugly Truck" and "Decorated Bicycle" entries, and awards that include "Most Ancient," "Most Horrible," and "Most Politically Incorrect." Politics, the environment, and social issues are big themes, whether that means poking fun at local and national politicians, mocking the profits of "Big Oil," or portraying a barrel-clad Uncle Sam as a down and outer. There are also a few Ancients and Horribles constants: a group of hairy, out-of-shape cross dressing men, and an entry satirizing the latest Hollywood blockbuster among them.

WATERFIRE

WaterFire has become the signature event of downtown Providence's revitalization. It consists of 100 fires that are lit in braziers in the middle of the rivers that converge on downtown around Waterplace Park. The event is the creation of artist Barnaby Evans, and the mix of fire, water, smoke and music is both mystical and inspiring.

Spectators line the waterways, some seated at prime restaurant patios, others milling about and watching the rippling water and flickering flames. WaterFire is staffed by an army of volunteers, including black-clad units who ply the rivers in small motor boats lighting the flames as darkness falls. Gondolas also make an appearance, resulting in an engaging combination of Pagan, European, Colonial and contemporary elements.

WaterFire is free, and is held on selected weekends during the warmer months. The event is at once always the same — fire and water — but also a little different each time as the music, crowd and weather changes. It's estimated that since its mid 1990s inception, WaterFire has been seen by ten million people.

TRINITY REP

Trinity Repertory Company was founded in 1963 and performs contemporary and classic works of drama for an audience of over 150,000 people yearly. The company is a rarity in that it features a long running and permanent stable of actors who must continually reinvent themselves with each production. Trinity has produced 54 world premieres, and has an annual budget of over eight million dollars.

Recent productions have included the world premiere *Shapeshifter*, as well as classics *The Importance of Being Earnest*, *A Raisin in the Sun* and *A Christmas Carol*, (which has been performed for more than 30 seasons). The company also trains actors and directors through its conservatory and its partnerships with Rhode Island College and Brown University. Trinity is located in the 1917 constructed Lederer Theater Center in the heart of downtown Providence, and is helmed by artistic director Curt Columbus. Previous artistic directors have included Oskar Eustis (now Artistic Director of New York's Public Theater) and 2008 Oscar Best Actor nominee Richard Jenkins.

BIG NAZO

Puppeteers extraordinaire Big Nazo feature huge other-worldly foam creations in all shapes, sizes and colors. Nazo characters include everything from oversized lab rats, robots and trolls, to go-go dancers and gargantuan carrots. There is also a Nazo band, a full-fledged ensemble featuring guitar, sax, and drums whose shows are packed with jokes, stunts, and audience participation.

Did you know. . .

that Newport is home to the International Tennis Hall of Fame? The Hall of Fame and museum (the world's largest devoted to tennis) was founded in 1954 and is located at the Newport Casino, site of the first US National Lawn Tennis Championships in 1881. This tournament has since come to be known as the US Open, and moved to Forest Hills, New York in 1915.

Did you know. . .

that the 2008 American League champion Tampa Devil Rays had two Rhode Islanders on their roster? Pitcher Dan Wheeler is a Warwick native and Pilgrim High School alumni, while outfielder Rocco Baldelli, who signed with the Boston Red Sox in January 2009, was born in Woonsocket and is a Bishop Hendricken grad. The '08 World Series champs, the Philadelphia Phillies, didn't field any players from Rhode Island, but their first base coach was East Providence-born Davey Lopes, a graduate of Providence's LaSalle Academy. Lopes was a MLB all-star second baseman in the 1970s and 80s known for his powerful bat and speed on the base paths.

In addition to putting on their own productions, Nazo has designed puppets for TV commercials and theatrical shows. Big Nazo have toured the world, and frequently play out-of-town festival gigs, but remain a frequent sight about the Ocean State, and maintain their headquarters and Nazo Lab in downtown Providence.

THE SPORTING LIFE

There is a rich tradition of high school, college and amateur sport in the state, as well as two pro teams: the Pawtucket Red Sox and the Providence Bruins. There are no Major League Baseball, NFL, NBA or NHL teams in Rhode Island, although Foxborough, Massachusetts, home of the NFL New England Patriots, is actually closer to Rhode Island than it is to Boston.

BASEBALL

The Pawtucket Red Sox have been the Boston Red Sox's AAA affiliate since 1973. It's a perfect fit: The parent club is less than an hour away, and Rhode Islanders are devout Red Sox fans, although abused Yankee partisans dot the landscape. The PawSox have been owned since 1977 by Ben Mondor, and since then the team has enjoyed considerable success on the field and at the gate. With Boston Red Sox tickets exorbitantly expensive, when obtainable at all, the PawSox represent a cost-friendly alternative for New England baseball fans.

McCoy Stadium has been home-field for a number of future Red Sox stars before they hit the bigs — Jim Rice, Wade Boggs, Kevin Youkilis and Dustin Pedroia among them. Many Red Sox players have also made brief stops in Pawtucket on injury rehab assignments. McCoy Stadium is in the record books as the scene of the longest game in professional baseball history: a 33-inning, eight-hour match between the PawSox and the Rochester Red Wings in 1981. Future Hall of Famer Cal Ripken came to bat 15 times for the Red Wings in the legendary contest.

In addition to the PawSox, there have been numerous professional, semi-pro, college, and amateur baseball clubs in the state. The best known is the Providence Grays, who played in the National League from 1878 to 1885, capturing an early version of the World Series in 1884 when they beat the New York Metropolitans of the American Association. The Grays, who played at Messer Street Grounds in Olneyville, had a record of 84-28 in 1878, with ace pitcher Charley Radbourn recording 59 of those wins.

FOOTBALL

Football in Rhode Island dates to the era when the game was played with a round ball. Brown University played its first game in November 1878, scrubbing up a squad to take on Amherst College who had graciously sent a letter requesting a match. None of the Brown players had ever seen a football game, so the team manager and captain journeyed to Cambridge, MA to observe the Harvard team and get some pointers. In the interim, a Providence tailor fashioned uniforms for the boys. The Bears failed to register a point in that first match, but in 1916 Brown made a trip to the Rose Bowl. Unfortunately, they were shut out there too.

The Bears' record over the years has been mixed, but Brown football has produced some notable alumni, including John Heisman (of Heisman Trophy fame) who played club football in the late 1880s, Fritz Pollard ('16) who was the first black NFL head coach, legendary Penn State coach Joe Paterno ('50), and Steve Jordan ('82), a six-time all-pro tight end as a member of the Minnesota Vikings. Rhode Islanders, football fans or not, will recognize the names of two other former Bears — governors Philip Noel ('54) and Don Carcieri ('65).

The University of Rhode Island also knows its way around a pig skin; its program began in 1895. The annual Brown-URI matchup for the Governor's Cup is the football highlight of year in the Ocean State. In addition to the college game, Providence was home to an early NFL squad, the Providence Steam Roller, who were league members from 1925 to 1931. The team played their games in the Cyclodome, a stadium built for bicycle racing. The Steam Roller won the NFL championship in 1928, and the Cyclodome was the site of the first night game in NFL history.

BASKETBALL

Rhode Island's greatest claim to athletic fame nationally is the Providence College Friars and University of Rhode Island Rams men's basketball programs.

The Friars, who play at the Dunkin' Donuts Center in downtown Providence, were established in 1926 and since then have racked up 23 seasons of 20 or more wins. The high water mark was a 28-win 1973-74 season when the Friars went to the Final Four under coach Dave Gavitt. Other Friars' coaches include Rick Pitino, who led the team to another Final Four appearance in 1987, and Joe Mullaney who coached the team from 1955-69, and then later from 1981-85. Friars' court legends are many, and include Lenny Wilkens ('60), Jimmy Walker ('67), Ernie DiGregorio ('73), Marvin Barnes ('74) and Ryan Gomes ('04).

The Rams, who play at the Ryan Center on the URI campus, started play in 1903 and had recorded 1335 wins against 986 losses through spring 2009. The Rams won 28 games in 1987-88, and have 18 seasons of 20 or more wins. Coaching legends include Frank Keaney, whose tenure lasted from 1920-48, and Ernie Calverley, a standout player in the mid-1940s who coached the team from 1957-68. Star Rams players over the years have included Steve Chubin ('66), Sly Williams ('79), Carlton Owens ('88) and Kenny Green ('90).

The Providence Steamrollers represent a footnote in Rhode Island basketball history. The Steamrollers were a pro team who were members of the Basketball Association of America (precursor to the NBA) for three losing seasons in the late 1940s. The team, which won a measly six games in 1946-47, folded after the 1948-49 season.

HOCKEY

The Ocean State was once home to the Rhode Island Reds, one of the most storied franchises in minor league hockey history. From 1926 until 1972, the Reds played at the much beloved (and now demolished) R.I. Auditorium on North Main Street in Providence. The team moved to the newly constructed Civic Center downtown in 1973, and folded four years later. In the era of the six-team NHL, the caliber of play in the minor leagues was high, and Rhode Island fans were treated to the exploits of such stars as forward Zellio Toppazzini, and goaltenders Harvey Bennett, Johnny Bower and Ed Giacomin.

Minor league hockey returned to the state in 1992 with the arrival of the Providence Bruins. The P-Bruins are the Boston Bruins American Hockey League (AHL) affiliate, and play at the Dunkin' Donuts Center. Center Patrice Bergeron and goaltender Tim Thomas are among current Boston standouts who have played for the P-Bruins.

The college game is popular in Rhode Island, notably the Providence College and Brown University teams. The PC squad dates to 1927, and the school has produced a number of NHL coaches and players. Lou Lamoriello, a Providence native, graduated from PC in 1963 and went on to coach hockey for 15 years at his alma mater. Lamoriello is the long time general manager and president of the New Jersey Devils of the NHL, and the team has won three Stanley Cups during his tenure. The cross-town Bears also started in the 1920s, and similarly have a number of alums playing in the NHL.

Remarkably, the most famous hockey team in Rhode Island just might be a bunch of high schoolers — the Mount Saint Charles Academy squad. The Woonsocket Catholic school is a hockey mecca, and draws players from thoughout the Northeast. Mount Saint Charles's alumni include a dozen or so current and former NHLers. Under legendary hard-nosed coach Bill Belisle, the team pulled off an unbelievable 26 consecutive Division 1 Boys Hockey championships between 1978 and 2003.

Weblinks

Providence Phoenix
www.thephoenix.com/providence
Alternative weekly with state-wide arts and entertainment listings.

Providence Journal
www.projo.com
See "Lifebeat" and "Event Calendar" tabs.

Newport Mercury
www.newportmercury.com
Newport area arts and entertainment.

Providence Online
www.providenceonline.com
Includes Providence Monthly, East Side Monthly and So Rhode Island listings.

Motif Magazine
www.motifmagazine.net
Twice-monthly arts and entertainment publication strong on music.

Rhode Island Monthly
www.rimonthly.com/
See "What's Happening" and "Travel & Leisure" tabs.

Rhode Island Roads
www.riroads.com
Rhody travel, dining, life, and entertainment.

Food

On a per square mile, per capita, or per bowl of pasta basis, it's hard to beat Rhode Island for food. The variety and quality are remarkable, whether it's a mini-mall sandwich shop, an ethnic restaurant, or a star chef's cutting-edge eatery. Moreover, Rhode Island, unlike many places in North America, has a genuine food culture in which food is not mere sustenance, but a vital part of the local fabric. Rhode Island's legendary seafood is a product of its coastal location, but equally, the state's waves of immigrants, particularly those from Italy, Quebec and Portugal, have been essential in defining Rhody cuisine.

A RHODE ISLAND FOOD GLOSSARY
Awful Awful®: A thick mixture of milk and ice cream sold at Newport Creamery restaurants ("Drink three get one free").

Bakery pizza: Sometimes called "pizza strips," it's a light and doughy thick crust pizza with tomato sauce and no cheese. Generally served at room temperature and found at neighborhood bakeries.

Cabinet: Cold milk blended with ice cream, elsewhere known as a milkshake. Delekta Pharmacy in Warren is the state's cabinet capital.

Cake donut: Also found outside the state, but Allie's Donuts of North Kingstown has legions of followers locally.

Cherry stones: Small quahogs.

Choggies: Ocean fish more widely known as cunner and common in Narragansett Bay.

Chowder (chowdah): Not unique to RI, but the three options of "red" (with a tomato based broth), "white" (with cream, what is typically considered clam chowder) and "clear" (clear broth) are an only-in-Rhody phenomena.

Clamcakes: Small pieces of quahog dipped in batter and deep fried.

Coffee milk: Milk with coffee syrup. Coffee milk is the state drink, and Autocrat coffee syrup the industry standard bearer.

Del's: Lemon slush drink, from the company of the same name.

Doughboy: Fried dough with powdered sugar, called *malasadas* in the Portuguese community.

Dynamite: Intense mix of meat sauce, green pepper and onions on a sub roll. Most common in Woonsocket, famously at the Castle Luncheonette on Social Street.

Family style chicken dinner: A family friendly *prix fixe* meal of baked chicken, pasta with red sauce, fries, rolls and salad. Popular in the Blackstone River Valley, notably at Wright's Farm Restaurant in Harrisville.

They said it

"Rhode Island has a surprising number of local dishes, food traditions, and culinary terms that are unique to the state—and none of them has ever strayed into the other New England states."

– Linda Beaulieu in her introduction to
The Providence and Rhode Island Cookbook.

Frappe: Cold milk mixed with ice cream, known as a milkshake elsewhere, and a cabinet locally.

Gravy: Italian tomato-based sauce served on pasta.

Grinder (grindah): A submarine sandwich.

Hot weiners: A local variant on the standard hot dog, sometimes called a "gagger."

Jonnycakes: Small pancakes made with stone-ground white flint cornmeal, unique to Rhode Island.

May breakfast: A community breakfast which dates to Revolutionary times in which churches and civic organizations open their doors to the public.

Meat pie: Also known as *tourtière*, this is a beef or pork pie with a flaky crust hailing originally from Quebec and found in the northern part of the state.

Milkshake: Cold milk flavored with syrup, but no ice cream.

Pogies: Ocean fish more widely known as menhaden, a kind of herring.

Quahog: Hard shelled clam, the official state shell. The name is derived from a Narragansett word, and is also spelled "quahaug."

Rare ripes: Scallions.

Stuffies: Bread/quahog mixture placed inside a quahog shell and baked.

TAKE 5   JOHNETTE RODGRIGUEZ'S FIVE ESSENTIAL RHODY FOODS (AND THE BEST PLACES TO FIND THEM)

Johnette Rodriguez has been writing on food and culture in Rhode Island and southern New England for over 20 years. Her articles and reviews frequently appear in *The Providence Phoenix, Yankee Magazine, Edible Rhody*, and *Balancing the Tides*. She has also been published in *The Boston Globe*.

1. **Jonnycakes: Jigger's Diner, 145 Main Street, East Greenwich**. The Rhode Island jonnycake wars between the East Bay and the West Bay are all about style — thin and made with cold milk, or thick and made with hot water? Jigger's (in the West Bay) are dense and chewy, made by pouring boiling water over stone-ground white-flint cornmeal. Eaten savory with fried eggs or sweet with maple syrup, these jonnycakes will definitely stick to your ribs.

2. **Clear Quahog Chowder: Commons Lunch, 48 Commons, Little Compton**. Most Rhode Islanders don't want their chowder sullied with milk. A base of straight clam juice broth, plus a few onions, potatoes, maybe some diced salt pork, and plenty of shucked quahogs (hard-shell clams) — that's chowder. Typical accompaniments are clam cakes or jonnycakes, both in good form at "the Commons."

Wandi: A traditional Italian cookie that is fried and sprinkled with confectioner's sugar.

Wimpy Skippy: A spinach pie with pepperoni and cheese available at Caserta's Pizza on Federal Hill in Providence.

Yacht Club Soda: Bottled in North Providence since 1915, comes in a variety of flavors.

3. **Stuffies (stuffed clams): Amaral's Fish & Chips, 4 Redmond Street, Warren**. Stuffies are to clams casino what steak is to chicken – they're large and hearty. Quahog shells are packed with chopped quahogs, bread and/or cracker crumbs, flavored with herbs and/or veggies and plenty of clam juice, often with a red pepper-flake kick to 'em. Amaral's have that kick but no green pepper, no bacon, no chourizo. Just the basics.

4. **Clam cakes (clam fritters): Flo's Clam Shack, 4 Wave Avenue, Middletown**. Rhode Island tradition has it that the clams are hard to find in clam cakes, but there's always a tang from the clam juice in the fritter-like batter. The trick is to keep the batter light and to deep-fry them so they come out dry and un-greasy. Flo's has been doing it for 69 years, so they've got it down.

5. **Fried calamari: Anthony's Seafood, 963 Aquidneck Avenue, Middletown**. The Rhode Island "state appetizer" of fried squid rings with pepperoncini slices and marinara sauce on the side comes in a superior incarnation at Anthony's. But this eatery also features a full dinner version, with fries and slaw, and a twist on the usual; Kung Pao calamari, tossed with lots of peanuts, scallions and plum chili sauce. A very East-meets-West kind of dish—and super-tasty!

BRING ME THE CHECK

- Number of RI eating and drinking establishments: 2,663
- 2008 sales: $1.9 billion
- Number of people employed in the food service industry: 51,500

Source: National Restaurant Association.

TAKE 5 TOP FIVE LEGENDARY WEINER JOINTS

1. **Olneyville New York System**. 20 Plainfield Street in the Olneyville area of Providence, also on Reservoir Avenue in Cranston and Mineral Spring Avenue in North Providence. A classic in the field since the 1930s, Olneyville sells their sauce by the packet and has been a filming location for the *Brotherhood* TV show.

2. **Original New York System**. 424 Smith Street in the Smith Hill area of Providence. Claims to be Rhode Island's original weiner shop (1927), although not surprisingly this distinction is in dispute. Salty proprietors, great sign, and wonderful weiners.

3. **Wein-O-Rama**. 1009 Oaklawn Avenue, Cranston. Proclaims that it is *not* a New York System, and is a cut above, although it does serve weiners with meat sauce. A Cranston tradition since 1962.

4. **Sparky's Coney Island System**. 122 Taunton Avenue, East Providence. Also lays claim to being the oldest weiner joint in the state (1915).

5. **Rod's Grille**. 6 Washington Street, Warren. Rod's debuted in 1955 and topped the "Best Greasy Spoon" category in the *Providence Phoenix* 2005 Reader's Poll.

DUNKIN' DONUTS

Dunkin' Donuts is headquartered in Massachusetts, but Rhode Island represents the spiritual seat of the empire. The first Rhode Island store opened in 1956 on North Main Street in Providence, and since then the chain (whose outlets are owned by franchisees) has steadily expanded, burrowing its way into cities, suburbs, and malls, even penetrating gas stations and grocery stores, the Bonanza Bus Terminal and T.F. Green Airport.

Despite its name, Dunkin' Donuts generates most of its sales from caffeinated beverages. It's doing a pretty good job; there are a total of 169 Dunkin' stores in the state; that's one for every 6,259 Rhode Islanders. By comparison, Starbucks has a measly 24 outlets, Honey Dew Donuts 32, and Tim Horton's (the Canadian juggernaut which purchased the defunct Bess Eaton donut store chain in 2004) 46. And Krispy Kreme? It opened a Cranston store to great fanfare in 2003, but by 2007 had closed its lone Rhode Island location.

As befits its dominant position, Dunkin' engages in overkill; in 2001 it purchased naming rights to the former Providence Civic Center. The arena is now known as the "Dunkin' Donuts Center" ("The Dunk" for short). Dunkin' Donuts is so much a part of Rhode Island life that it seems unremarkable, a fact of nature almost. One thing that is not natural, however, is the Rhody maneuver of sipping a Dunkin' Donuts coffee while changing lanes (no surprise that a signal isn't given) and yakking on the phone.

Did you know. . .

that the White Horse Tavern in Newport is one of North America's oldest such establishments? The building was constructed as a residence in 1652, and converted to a tavern in 1673. In its early days, when it was operated by a pirate, it served as meeting place for the Colony's General Assembly, Criminal Court and City Council. The contemporary version of the White Horse Tavern consistently ranks among Rhode Island's top restaurants.

TAKE 5 RICHARD GUTMAN'S FIVE
QUINTESSENTIAL RHODE ISLAND DINERS

Richard J.S. Gutman is director and curator of the Culinary Arts Museum at Johnson & Wales University's Harborside Campus. He is the author of several books on diners, including *American Diner Then and Now* and *The Worcester Lunch Car Company*.

1. **Haven Brothers Diner**. Fulton Street at City Hall, Providence. The diner is pulled by truck into downtown Providence every evening by dusk, and continues the tradition of fast food on wheels that began in Providence in 1872.

2. **The Modern Diner**. 364 East Avenue, Pawtucket. The Modern is a bullet-nosed streamliner, locked in the landscape but looking like a locomotive that's about to blast off along some imaginary steel rails. This historic 1941 building (one of only two of its style still operating) has the distinction of being the first roadside diner listed on the National Register of Historic Places.

3. **The Seaplane Diner**. 307 Allens Avenue, Providence. The Seaplane is hard to spot in its industrial setting — which is hard to imagine since it is clad in horizontal stripes of gleaming stainless steel and glinting blue glass. The Seaplane is the second diner on this site, and the present building was trucked in from Woonsocket as a used diner in 1975 when the previous one proved too small for its booming business.

4. **Bishop's 4th Street Diner**. 184 Admiral Kalbfus Road, Newport. Don't let the name fool you. It's located just off the rotary where Connell Highway intersects Admiral Kalbfus. A great 1950s diner in near-original condition. Despite the Newport address, it serves classic diner eats with a Portuguese touch at moderate prices. Many tout its biscuits and gravy.

5. **The Liberty Elm**. 777 Elmwood Avenue, Providence. The latest incarnation of a diner built in 1947 has seen nearly as many owners as customers darken its doors. Now it serves fresh, sustainable food, washed down by fair-trade coffee or Yacht Club locally-made soda. Its back-room addition is a venue for live music on Sundays, and doubles as a wireless café always.

Did you know...

that celebrity chef Emeril Lagasse is a 1978 graduate of Johnson & Wales University's Culinary Arts program? Johnson & Wales has one of the top such programs in the nation, and the J & W contingent brought home four medals from the 2008 Culinary Olympics held in Germany.

FAST FOOD
International Chains:
- Number of McDonalds: 29 (over 13,000 in US)
- Number of Subways: 73 (about 22,000 in US)
- Number of Burger Kings: 25 (about 7,000 in US)

LOCAL FAMILY RESTAURANT CHAINS
Newport Creamery: Founded as a dairy in 1928 in Newport, now owned by the Jan Companies and headquartered in Cranston. Eleven Rhode Island locations "At the Sign of the Golden Cow": Barrington, Middletown, Providence, Coventry, Greenville, Newport, Cranston, Johnston, North Kingstown, Warwick, Warwick Mall.

Chelo's Hometown Bar & Grill: Founded in 1955, headquartered in Cumberland. Ten locations: Woonsocket, Greenville (Apple Valley Mall), Rumford (Newport Ave), Providence, East Providence, Cranston, Warwick (Post Road), Warwick Mall, Warwick (Greenwich Bay) and Wakefield.

Gregg's Restaurants & Pubs: Founded in 1972, headquartered in Warwick. Four locations: Providence, East Providence, Warwick and North Kingstown.

Did you know...

that baking powder was invented and first manufactured in Rhode Island? Rumford Chemical Works of East Providence began producing baking powder for sale in 1869.

FEDERAL HILL

Federal Hill is the go-to place for Italian food in Rhode Island, and a big draw with locals and visitors alike. The Hill is known for such venerable Italian restaurants as Angelo's, Camille's and Joe Marzilli's Old Canteen, as well as newer entries, including Sienna, Cassarino's and Zooma. There is a range of options on Federal Hill as modest pizza places and sandwich shops sit next to pricy sommelier staffed establishments. All told, there are about 35 restaurants on the Hill, mostly, although not exclusively, on Atwells avenue.

TAKE 5 GAYOT'S TOP RHODE ISLAND RESTAURANTS

1. **Al Forno**, 577 South Main, Providence. Top of the line regional Italian and Mediterranean cuisine using local ingredients.
2. **The Dining Room at the Castle Hill Inn & Resort**, 590 Ocean Avenue, Newport. Varied and exquisite menu with spectacular ocean views.

FIVE WAY TIE FOR 3RD:
3. **Agora, The Westin Providence**, 1 Exchange Place, Providence. Beautiful surroundings and lush contemporary cuisine.
4. **Café Nuovo**, 1 Citizen's Plaza, Providence. Views of the Providence River and legendary deserts.
5. **New Rivers Restaurant**, 7 Steeple Street, Providence. Multi-ethnic cuisine in a warm ambience.
6. **Siena Restaurant**, 238 Atwells Avenue, Providence. Tuscan classics and New England seafood in a lively Federal Hill setting.
7. **The Spiced Pear**, Chanler Hotel, 117 Memorial Boulevard, Newport. Elegant gourmet dining among the Newport Mansions.

Source: Gayot.com.

Italian spots dominate, but there are also Asian, Mexican and contemporary American restaurants, plus various bars, lounges, and cafés. In addition to the restaurants, legendary stops on Atwells include Tony's Colonial Food Store, Venda Ravioli (a gourmet Italian food emporium) and Scialo Bros. Bakery. The following are likely when visiting the Hill: parking will be murder, you'll eat too much and come away with a Buddy Cianci sighting.

NEW YORK SYSTEM

A sign reading "Hot Weiners New York System" is definitely a head scratcher for the visitor or newcomer to Rhode Island — the weiner part makes sense, but what is the system and how does New York fit in? Well, there is no "system" *per se*, and the "New York" tag was originally used by Greek immigrants who came to Rhode Island via NYC, and used "New York" to lend authenticity to their product. Essentially, a New York System (which is not for the faint of stomach) is a weiner with spicy meat sauce.

The Rhody weiner is not a regular hot dog — it's smaller, has tapered ends, and is fried on a griddle rather than being boiled or steamed. The sauce, without which the weiner experience is rather tame, is a combination of ground beef, onions, garlic and other spices. The various New York Systems fiercely guard their own particular sauce recipe, but the weiners themselves are fairly standard, and are served on a steamed bun.

Order a weiner and the counter person will ask if you want it "all the way," which means with sauce, mustard, celery salt and chopped

Did you know...

that Chan's, a Woonsocket Chinese restaurant that dates to 1905, is a leading venue for jazz and blues concerts? Chan's attracts both touring and local acts, including ace blues guitarist (and Woonsocket native) Duke Robillard.

onions. Because the weiners are smaller than a typical dog, diners usually order several at a time, and the weiner man, if a traditionalist, will line them "up the ahm" (his, not yours) as he prepares the delicacies. It is customary, although not mandatory, to wash down weiners with coffee milk. Weiner joints aren't just for kids, and many are open to the wee hours, capturing both second shift workers and revelers on their way home after a night on the town.

FINE DINING
Since the early 1990s there has been an explosion of innovative and stylish restaurants in Rhode Island. Providence in particular has seen so many new places pop up that's it hard to believe that the area can support them all, and it doesn't, as periodically a hot spot goes under, but is then soon replaced by the next big thing.

Did you know. . .

that restaurant consultant Bill Tribelli, a Culinary Arts instructor at the Rhode Island Training School and Adult Correctional Institute, is author of the 2004 book *Jailhouse Cooking: The Poor Man's Guide To Cooking*?

Did you know. . .

that the Cuisinart was designed by former RISD instructor Marc Harrison? Harrison (1936-1998) was a proponent of "Universal Design" which attempts to make products accessible to the elderly and disabled, thereby making them easy for everyone to use. The Cuisinart's big and easily manipulated buttons have made it an enduring kitchen staple.

Al Forno, which opened in Providence in 1980, is generally credited with kicking off the fine dining binge and putting the state on the map with foodies. Chef/owners Johanne Killeen and George Germon's innovative approach to Italian regional cooking has been lauded in pretty much every major style and food magazine. The duo, who are credited with inventing grilled pizza, have garnered many awards, and have written two books: *Cucina Simpatica* (1991) and *On Top of Spaghetti* (2006).

DEL'S

Del's is Rhode Island's ultimate summertime drink. It originated in 1948 in Cranston when founder Angelo DeLucia took an old family recipe from Italy involving snow, lemons and sugar, and concocted his much beloved slushy treat. The characteristic green, white and yellow carts, vans and drive-up windows are now ubiquitous throughout the state. Del's, which implores prospective customers to "Stop at the Sign of the Lemon," has burst beyond Rhode Island's borders, and is found in a total of 14 states, mostly in the Northeast, but also in Nevada, where a number of casinos feature the famous Rhody slush.

Did you know. . .

that the Rhode Island Community Food Bank feeds over 40,000 Rhode Islanders monthly and distributes over eight million pounds of food a year?

SUDS

Narragansett Brewing Company was founded in 1888, and by the 1950s was the dominant beer in New England. It sponsored the Boston Red Sox, and was famous for its "Hi Neighbor. Have a Gansett" slogan. The good times didn't last however, and Narragansett, which used water from the Scituate Reservoir to supply its Cranston brewery, was sold in the 1960s and fell into decline. The Cranston plant was shuttered in 1983, and brewing operations transferred to Indiana.

Narragansett was corpse-like until 2005 when East Providence native and former Nantucket Nectars President Mark Hellendrung purchased the brand and restarted the company. Narragansett Lager is now brewed in Rochester, NY, and the Bock and Porter beers are made locally at Trinity Brew House. While not as popular as it was decades ago, Narragansett is again a staple in Rhode Island liquor stores, bars and restaurants. And, ironically for a brand once associated with aging blue collar suburbanites, its tall cans are now a popular barroom choice amongst budget conscious students and hipsters.

Narragansett might be a revived classic, but Newport Storm is a thoroughly contemporary one. Founded in 1999 and based in Middletown, Newport Storm's flagship beer is Hurricane Amber Ale, but it also brews a range of seasonal and specialty beers. Newport Storm is widely available in Rhode Island, and is gaining a toehold outside the state.

Fine beer certainly isn't limited to Newport County, and Providence's Trinity Brewhouse is the state's largest brewer. It has won

Did you know. . .

that Rhode Island is home to six wineries? There are vineyards in Coventry, Cumberland, Westerly, Portsmouth, Middletown, and Little Compton. The Coastal Wine Trail of Southeastern New England (www.coastalwinetrail.com) takes in the latter four wineries, plus three more in neighboring Massachusetts.

numerous awards, and makes a range of ales, stouts, porters and other brews. A downtown landmark, Trinity Restaurant and Brewery serves food until midnight, and drinks until at least one a.m. seven days a week.

Weblinks

Edible Rhody
www.ediblerhody.com/content
"A quarterly journal that celebrates local food, season by season, and tells the stories of the farmers, chefs, fishers and food artisans who work and live in Rhode Island."

Tasteri.com
www.tasteri.com
Restaurant reviews from *Rhode Island Monthly* critic Karen Deutsch and others, as well as *Providence Journal* reviewers. See also www.rimonthly.com.

Providence Journal Food Section
www.projo.com
Rhode Island food guru Gail Ciampa anchors the weekly Wednesday round-up of reviews, recipes, features and notes about cooking and dining in Rhode Island.

Culinary Archives & Museum at Johnson & Wales University
www.culinary.org
One of the nation's top cooking schools hosts a museum that includes exhibits on everything from diners and nineteenth century New England taverns, to White House menus and a 120-pound 1960s era microwave.

Providence Monthly & East Side Monthly
www.providenceonline.com
Restaurant reviews by Linda Beaulieu and others.

Economy

Rhode Island was founded by religious exiles, not wealth seekers, and in its early years was a modest agricultural settlement. By the 1700s, however, Rhode Island had become a center for the shipping trade, and Newport, Bristol and Providence were busy ports. Following the American Revolution, the locus of the economy shifted toward industry, and the state's northern cities became major goods producers, with textiles and metals related manufacturers leading the way. In the twentieth century, and particularly in the post WWII era, manufacturing declined in importance and many of Rhode Island's sprawling factories were shuttered.

Manufacturing now accounts for around ten percent of Rhode Island employment, well behind health care and social assistance. The shift toward a service economy is not unique to Rhode Island, but the very large share of jobs and wealth once concentrated in manufacturing has made for a difficult transition. Nonetheless, Rhode Island's economy is diverse, with the exception of very small agriculture and mining sectors, unsurprising given the state's size and location.

GDP

Gross domestic product represents the total value of goods and services produced in the economy.

- Total RI GDP (2007): $46.9 billion
- RI GDP per capita in 2000 dollars (2007): $36,543
- New England GDP per capita in 2000 dollars (2007): $44,603
- US GDP per capita in 2000 dollars (2007): $38,020

Source: US Bureau of Economic Analysis.

TAXES

- State sales tax: 7 percent
- Personal income tax rate: 3.75 percent on the first $32, 549 of taxable income; 7.0 percent on the amount between $32,550 and $78,849; 7.75 percent on the amount between $78,850 and $164,549; 9.0 percent on the amount between $164,550 and $357,699 and 9.9 percent on amounts over $357,700.
- Business corporation tax rate: 9 percent of net income.

Source: State of Rhode Island (2008).

TAX FREEDOM DAY

Tax freedom day is the date on which earnings no longer go to taxes. It is calculated by dividing total taxes collected by total income. Selected "Freedom days" are listed below.

Alaska: March 29 (earliest in the nation)

New Hampshire: April 15

United States: April 23

Rhode Island: April 24

Florida: April 26

Connecticut: May 8 (last in the nation)

Source: Tax Foundation.

TAKE 5 FIVE RHODE ISLAND
SALARIES

1. **Don Carcieri, Governor, State of Rhode Island:** $119,818
2. **Jim Baron, URI men's basketball coach:** $310,246
3. **Ruth Simmons, President, Brown University:** $775,718
4. **George Vecchione, CEO, Lifespan health system** (comprises Rhode Island, Hasbro Children's, Miriam, Newport and Bradley Hospitals): $2.95 million total compensation and benefits
5. **Thomas Ryan, CEO CVS/Caremark:** $18 million – includes salary, bonuses, stock and other compensation

INCOME

Rhode Island's per capita disposable personal income (total personal income minus taxes) was $34,894 in 2007. This amount is higher than the US average of $33, 619, but substantially less than New England's figure of $40,066. Selected state figures:

Alabama: $28,960

Iowa: $31,020

Vermont: $33,156

California: $35,666

Massachusetts: $41,491

Source: US·Bureau Economic Analysis.

Did you know. . .

that 5,900 people were employed producing jewelry and silverware in November 2008 in Rhode Island? While still an important sector, as recently as 1978, jewelry and silverware production had employed 33,000 workers.

TAKE 5 FIVE ITEMS NOT SUBJECT TO RI SALES TAX

1. Sales in public buildings by blind people.
2. Sale of compressed air.
3. Sale of a new or used boat.
4. Sale of horse food products to persons engaged in the business of boarding horses.
5. Sales of United States, Rhode Island or POW-MIA flags.

Source: State of Rhode Island.

SHOW ME THE MONEY

Average annual private sector salaries (2007)

Maine: $34,461

Vermont: $36,351

Rhode Island: $39,827

New Hampshire: $44,308

US: $44,355

Massachusetts: $55,819

Connecticut: $59,174

Source: Rhode Island Department of Labor and Training.

Did you know. . .

that Lincoln-based A.T. Cross, the United States' oldest manufacturer of precision writing instruments, supplied the pen that Barack Obama used to sign inauguration documents? Cross was founded in 1846 in Providence, and is credited with, among other inventions, the development of the 1879 Stylographic pen, a forerunner to the ball point.

EMPLOYMENT BY SECTOR
Sector and percentage of total:
- Healthcare & Social Assistance: 16.3
- Government: 13.3
- Professional & Business Services: 11.2
- Retail Trade: 10.0
- Manufacturing: 9.7
- Accommodation & Food Services: 9.1
- Financial Activities: 7.0
- Educational Services: 5.0
- Other Services: 4.8
- Construction: 4.0
- Wholesale Trade: 3.5
- Transportation & Utilities: 2.8
- Information: 2.2

Source: Rhode Island Department of Labor & Training (2009).

TAKE 5 FIVE LARGEST
PRIVATE SECTOR EMPLOYERS (2008)

Excludes government, healthcare, social services and educational/religious institutions.

1. **CVS Caremark.** Retail pharmacy. Headquarters: Woonsocket, RI.
2. **Citizens Financial Group** (Royal Bank of Scotland). Banking. Headquarters: Scotland, UK.
3. **Stop & Shop Supermarket Co (Royal Ahold)**. Retail grocery. Headquarters: Quincy, MA.
4. **Bank of America**. Banking. Headquarters: Charlotte, NC.
5. **Fidelity Investments**. Financial Services. Headquarters: Boston, MA.

Source: Rhode Island Economic Development Corporation.

TAKE 5 FIVE KEY RHODE ISLAND
HEADQUARTERED COMPANIES

1. **CVS/Caremark**. The Woonsocket-based drug and healthcare behemoth ranked number 24 on the Fortune 500 with $73.6 billion in annual revenues in 2007. The company has 6,300 stores and fills or manages a billion prescriptions annually. CVS employs 190,000 people, and in 2007 merged with Caremark Rx, a pharmacy benefit management company. CVS (which stands for Customer Value Stores) began in 1963 with one Lowell, MA retail store. It has been on an acquisitions binge of late, buying up drug store chains including Sav-On, Osco and Eckerd.

2. **Textron**. Headquartered in Providence, Textron was founded as a textile company in 1923. It ranked number 202 on the Fortune 500 with 2007 revenues of $13.2 billion. The company employs 42,000 in 28 countries, and is best known for its aircraft and defense industry products. Textron brands include Bell Helicopter and Cessna Aircraft.

3. **Hasbro**. Founded in 1923 as a textile remnant company, Hasbro had 2007 worldwide net revenues of $3.8 billion. It produced its first toy, the iconic Mr. Potato Head, in the 1940s. Since then, Pawtucket based Hasbro has developed many other toys and games, as well as buying companies and brands including Tonka, Playskool, Parker Brothers, Milton Bradley and Cranium Inc.

4. **FM Global**. The Johnston-based company specializes in commercial insurance and risk management and prevention. FM Global's roots date to 1835 when textile mill owner Zachariah Allen made improvements to his factory to reduce the risk of fire. He asked for a reduction in his premiums, and receiving none, formed an insurance company with other like-minded mill owners. The company retains a focus on research and engineering based reductions in risk, and had a 2007 net income of $928 million.

5. **Nortek**. Established in 1967, Providence-headquartered Nortek is a privately held commercial and residential building products manufacturer. Nortek and subsidiaries produce a range of items including bath and kitchen fans, and home ventilation and security systems. Nortek reported net sales of $2.4 billion and net earnings of $32.4 million in 2007.

YOU SAID HOW MUCH?

All figures are median hourly wages and are drawn from the most recently available data from the Rhode Island Department of Labor and Training.

Family & general practitioners: $84.53 (mean)
Psychiatrists: $82.21 (mean)
Chief executives: $80.82 (mean)
Pharmacists: $46.19
Lawyers: $41.06
Economists: $38.65
Electrical engineers: $37.55
Accountants & auditors: $28.79
Detectives & criminal investigators: $28.08
Librarians: $27.86
Captains, mates and pilots of water vessels: $22.67
Fire fighters: $22.33
Postal service mail carriers: $21.61
Graphic designers: $20.86
Computer support specialists: $20.50
Animal trainers: $19.06
Clergy: $18.49
Highway maintenance workers: $17.51
Tree trimmers & pruners: $17.08
Butchers & meat cutters: $16.75
Model makers, metal & plastic: $14.26
Textile bleaching & dyeing machine operators: $13.93
Pest control workers: $13.87
Jewelers & precious stone & metal workers: $12.97
Bakers: $12.85
Retail salespeople: $10.55
Sewers, hand: $9.02
Food servers: $7.90

They said it

"*Contrary to what our leaders would have us believe, most of our state's current economic problems are not the result of national economic weakness. While no one individual is directly responsible, our present problems were brought on by ineffective overall economic leadership during the past 20 years in general (since Rhode Island became a post-manufacturing economy), and the last 10 years in particular.*"

– **University of Rhode Island economics professor Leonard Lardaro, Ph.D., writing in the *Providence Journal* in January 2008.**

MINIMUM WAGE

Rhode Island's minimum wage as of January 2007 was $7.40; in 1956 it was $0.90. The federal minimum wage as of July 2007 was $5.85.

Did you know. . .

that travel and tourism generates more than $3.6 billion for the Rhode Island economy? According to the Rhode Island Tourism Division, the tourism and hospitality industry supports over 80,000 jobs.

Did you know. . .

that in 2008 there were two Rhode Islanders on *Forbes* magazine's list of the 400 richest Americans? Jonathan Nelson of Providence, founder and CEO of Providence Equity Partners, ranked number 227, and Middletown's Hope Hill van Beuren, heiress to the Campbell Soup fortune, was number 355.

TAKE 5 HASBRO TOYS
IN FIVE CATEGORIES

1. **Characters:** G.I. Joe, My Little Pony, Mr. Potato Head
2. **Board games:** Monopoly, Trivial Pursuit, Clue, Yahtzee, Candy Land, Scrabble, Dungeons & Dragons
3. **Building/creating:** Easy-Bake Oven, Tinker Toy Construction Set
4. **Big screen stars:** Transformers, Star Wars
5. **Active:** Nerf, Twister, Lazer Tag, U-Dance

POVERTY

According to the US Census Bureau, 12 percent of Rhode Islanders were living below the poverty level in 2007 (the figure for the US as a whole was 13 percent). Rhode Island's child poverty rate in 2007 was 17 percent, and over 30 percent of kids in Providence, Central Falls and Woonsocket were classified as poor. The federal poverty measure, however, is widely judged to be unrealistic for the urban Northeast, as the figure for a family of four with two children was $20,651 in 2007. A good chunk of this amount would be eaten up by Rhode Island's high housing costs, before any other expenses were factored in.

The Poverty Institute at the Rhode Island College of Social Work takes into account the actual cost of living in the state in developing its

Did you know...

that Ashaway Line and Twine Mfg. Co., located in the Hopkinton village of Ashaway, is the longest-running family business in the US? The firm was founded in 1824 by Captain Lester Crandall as a manufacturer of fishing line, and is now a leading producer of strings for racket sports as well as surgical suture thread.

"The whole state is 1,000 square miles with 1 million people in it and we all know each other — in an innovation economy, that's a huge advantage. Connecting the dots across sectors and silos is what innovation is all about, and we have the perfect real world test bed."

– Saul Kaplan, former Executive Director of the Rhode Island Economic Development Corporation, on the evolution of Providence as a high tech center.

"Rhode Island Standard of Need" (RISN). In 2008, the RISN figure for a single adult was $20,280, for a single parent with two small children $47,352, and for a two-parent family with two small children $52,188. The Poverty Institute notes that a Rhode Island family of four needs gross earnings of 275 percent of the federal poverty level, or more than $58,000, to meet its basic needs without government assistance.

THE HIGHS AND LOWS

In 2000, *Money* magazine rated Providence the best place to live in the Northeast. The magazine cited Providence's quality of life, as well as its affordability and safety relative to other cities in the region. Unfortunately, in 2008, *Forbes* magazine ranked Providence the ninth most stressful city in the nation, noting the city's high unemployment, high population density and high cost of living.

Did you know...

that according to 2008 Bureau of Labor Statistics figures, 16.5 percent of Rhode Island's public and private sector workforce is unionized, the second highest rate in New England? The rate for the US as a whole is 12.4 percent. Connecticut is tops in New England with a 16.9 percent rate of workforce unionization, while New Hampshire is lowest at 10.6 percent.

TAKE 5 FIVE LARGEST EMPLOYERS
(2008)

1. **Rhode Island State Government:** (does not include public college employees); 15,978 employees
2. **Lifespan health system:** Healthcare, includes Rhode Island and other hospitals; 11,772 employees
3. **US Government:** (excluding military); 9,700 employees
4. **Roman Catholic Diocese of Providence:** Religious and educational (includes teachers employed by Catholic Schools of Rhode Island); 6,200 employees
5. **Care New England:** Healthcare, includes Women & Infants Hospital of RI and Kent County Memorial Hospital, among others; 6,193 employees

Source: Rhode Island Economic Development Corporation.

WORKING FOR UNCLE SAM

About 62,000 Rhode Islanders work in the public sector, about 13 percent of state employment.
• Percentage who work for local governments: 57
• Percentage who work for state government: 27
• Percentage who work for the federal government: 16

Source: Rhode Island Economic Development Corporation.

Did you know. . .

that imports from China are nothing new? From the late 1700s to the mid-1800s, over 75 voyages were made between Narragansett Bay and China for trading purposes. The first one left Rhode Island in 1787 and took 10 months to reach its destination. It returned in 1789 carrying $100,000 worth of goods.

TAKE 5 JOSH MILLER'S TOP FIVE THINGS
A RHODE ISLAND BUSINESS PERSON
SHOULD CARE ABOUT (OTHER THAN TAXES)

Providence restaurateur Josh Miller is owner and founder of the award-winning Trinity Brewhouse, and is also a partner in the bar Hot Club and the owner of Local 121, a restaurant/bar. Local 121, which opened in 2007, features regionally grown food and occupies the ground floor of the former Dreyfus Hotel in downtown Providence. Miller has served as President of the Downtown Providence Merchant's Association, as well as board member for Farm Fresh Rhode Island, the Providence Warwick Convention & Visitors Bureau, and the Rhode Island Economic Development Corporation. Cranston resident Miller is also the state Senator for District 28 (Cranston, Warwick) in the Rhode Island General Assembly.

1. **Health Care/Insurance Reform**. For most employers, health care benefits are one of the major expenses of doing business. Federal or state reforms relieving the burden on employers will provide significantly more relief to the bottom line than any potential tax code changes.

2. **Renewable Energy Initiatives**. Not only the fastest way to lower (or slow the increase) of utility bills, but potentially one of the fastest job creators.

3. **Increased Aid to Education**. Means property tax relief. A predictable statewide formula for funding education, as well as district consolidation and increased federal aid, would result in savings to property owners and an improved system producing a better educated workforce.

4. **An Infrastructure Strategy that Includes Improving Public Transportation**. Creates jobs and gets workers to them.

5. **Buy Local**. Try to find a Rhode Island source for EVERYTHING you purchase, or service you use. Need I explain this one?

TAKE 5 FIVE LEAST EXPENSIVE
MUNICIPALITIES IN WHICH TO BUY A HOUSE

Median sale price of a single-family house in 2008

1. **Providence** (excluding East Side) $123,500
2. **Central Falls** $142,000
3. **Pawtucket** $177,000
4. **Woonsocket** $180,000
5. **Warwick** $193,000

Source: Rhode Island Association of Realtors.

THE COMMUTE

Rhode Islanders spend an average of 22.3 minutes getting to work; the US average is 25 minutes. The nation's easiest commute is in North Dakota, where it takes 15.5 minutes to get to the job. New York State has the nation's toughest slog at 30.9 minutes, closely followed by Maryland at 30.6 minutes. And how do Rhode Islanders get to work?

- 81.1 percent drive alone
- 8.9 percent car/van/truck pool
- 2.6 percent use public transit
- 3.0 percent walk
- 1.8 percent use a cab, bicycle, motorcycle or other means
- 2.7 percent work at home

Source: Bureau of Transportation Statistics.

Did you know. . .

that the national debt is over eleven trillion dollars? You would if you drove past the Greenwood residence on Sayles Avenue in Pawtucket. William and David Greenwood post the total amount of the debt on a wooden board affixed to the side of their house, updating it weekly.

THE CRISIS THIS TIME

By early 2009, Rhode Island's unemployment rate exceeded ten percent, among the highest in the country. The avalanche of new requests for jobless benefits left claimants on hold with the Department of Labor and Training (DLT) for hours, if they could get through at all.

The labor force, which includes job holders and job seekers, was down 10,500 in 2008, indicating many had given up looking for work, or had left the state. If discouraged job searchers and the underemployed — those working part-time but wanting to work full-time — are added to the state's officially unemployed, the jobs picture appears even bleaker.

The poor employment situation has been coupled with declining real estate values, particularly in poorer urban areas where there have been many foreclosures. Other negative indicators include a drop in retail sales, and a decline in per capita income. Moreover, a number of Rhode Island's municipalities are confronting serious deficits, causing lay-offs of teachers, fire fighters, police officers and other city employees.

Rhode Island's economic downturn started in early 2007, and the global financial meltdown which hit in the fall of 2008 exacerbated the situation. The housing bubble's collapse rippled through the Rhode Island economy, causing job losses in construction, professional and business services, and retail sales. There has also been a loss of manufacturing jobs, a trend which has been ongoing for decades. The current crisis isn't the first time in recent memory the state has experienced tough economic times — the early 1990s in the wake of the banking crisis was another low period, as was the early 1980s when unemployment reached 9.7 percent.

It would be nice to think that since Rhode Island preceded the national economy into the current downturn it will emerge earlier, but economists are generally gloomy about the state's future. Rhode Island's residents concur; a 2008 Gallup poll ranked Rhode Island last in the country in terms of its residents' level of confidence in the economy.

Rhode Island's economy suffers from structural problems, not just a downturn in the business cycle. Broadly speaking, the state has a less

TAKE 5 FIVE MOST EXPENSIVE
MUNICIPALITIES IN WHICH TO BUY A HOUSE

(Median sale price of a single-family house in 2008)

1. **Little Compton**	$651,750
2. **Jamestown**	$525,000
3. **East Side of Providence**	$486,000
4. **East Greenwich**	$465,000
5. **Narragansett**	$410,100

Source: Rhode Island Association of Realtors.

skilled, educated, productive and wealthy workforce than neighboring Massachusetts and Connecticut. However, doing business in Rhode Island is sufficiently expensive that the state can't compete on price with low-cost areas. Rhode Island also has a less quantifiable deficit in confidence and vision — locals tend to think the worst about the state and its prospects, thereby inhibiting investment and other useful activity.

GENDER GAP

In 2007, women's median earnings in Rhode Island were 77.3 percent those of men. The figure for the US as a whole was 77.5 percent. Among the New England states, Vermont had the greatest parity with women earning 84.1 percent of men's wages, while New Hampshire had the least with women taking home 69.5 percent of men's earnings.

Did you know...

that the Tax Foundation ranked Rhode Island number 46 in state business tax climate for fiscal year 2009? Wyoming, South Dakota and Nevada were the top three, while the bottom four were Ohio, California, New York and New Jersey. South Carolina was in the middle of the pack at number 25.

The American Industrial Revolution

In 1793, English immigrant Samuel Slater kicked off the American Industrial Revolution when he built a water-powered cotton spinning mill on the banks of the Blackstone River in Pawtucket. Other mills sprouted along the Blackstone and other rivers, as did company sponsored mill villages. During the 1800s, the mills produced great wealth, but were famous for their low wages, harsh conditions, and use of child labor.

Cotton milling began to decline as early as the late 1800s; operations in the southern states received greater investment (sometimes from Rhode Island companies) and had lower labor costs. Rhode Island became dominant in the production of woolens, and in 1900, Providence was the country's chief producer of woolen and worsted goods. By the 1920s, however, Rhode Island was no longer a leader in the textile trade, woolen or cotton. The business received a bump from 1940s wartime demand, but in the post WWII era, textile production continued to slide and became a negligible part of the economy.

The mill era was crucial in shaping the state as it led to the construction of the Blackstone Canal (operational from 1828 to 1848) and the Providence Worcester Railroad, which opened in 1848. There were also numerous bridges, roads and other infrastructure that were built to serve the factories and their workers. Moreover, the mills attracted many people to Rhode Island, transforming it into an industrial, urban and multiethnic state.

Textiles were Rhode Island's first industry, but the state was far from a one trick pony. Rhode Island became famous for the manufacture of metal goods, jewelry, and rubber products. Providence was known for its "Five Industrial Wonders of the World": Browne & Sharpe (the world's largest tool factory), Nicholson File (the largest file factory), Corliss (the largest steam engine factory), American Screw (the largest screw factory) and Gorham (the largest silverware factory). In addition to the big manufacturing firms, in the 1800s and early 1900s there were thousands of smaller factories and workshops in and around Providence producing a range of household, commercial and industrial goods.

They said it

"Paper money will invariably operate in the body of politics as spirit liquors on the human body. They prey on the vitals and ultimately destroy them. Paper money has had the effect in your state that it will ever have, to ruin commerce, oppress the honest, and open the door to every species of fraud and injustice."

**– George Washington weighing in on the adoption
of paper money in 1787 correspondence with
Jabez Brown, Deputy Governor of Rhode Island.**

HOME SWEET HOME

The roller coaster metaphor for the Rhode Island housing market is certainly apt. After declining from 1989 to 1994, median prices for single-family houses increased steadily from $115,000 in 1995 to a peak of $285,000 in 2006. They have since fallen dramatically. The median price in February 2009 for a single family house was $185,000, down 26 percent from the $249,000 median price recorded a year earlier. Houses are sitting on the market longer as well, and there were 12.5 percent fewer houses sold in 2008 than 2007. The 2008 foreclosure rate was over 15 times that of 2006, and Rhode Island has a greater subprime dollar share of home loans than the US as a whole. House prices are expected to continue declining until 2011.

Sources: Providence Journal, Freddie Mac, Rhode Island Association of Realtors.

Did you know. . .

that Cumberland Farms convenience stores had their origin in Cumberland in 1939 when Greek immigrants Vasilios and Aphrodite Haseotes established a dairy farm? In the 1950s, the couple opened a store in Bellingham, Massachusetts, and the chain established itself throughout the Northeast in the 1960s. Gas pumps were added to the mix in 1971, and "Cumbies" now has over 1,000 gas and convenience store outlets in the Northeast and Florida. The Canton, Massachusetts headquartered company employs 7,000 people.

TAKE 5   TOM SGOUROS'S TOP FIVE
MYTHS ABOUT THE RHODE ISLAND
POLITICAL ECONOMY

Tom Sgouros is the editor of the Rhode Island Policy Reporter (RIPR), a newsletter, column and website devoted to local, state and federal policy issues affecting life in the Ocean State. RIPR examines what government actually does (instead of what politicians say) in areas such as taxation, education, immigration, and healthcare policy. Sgouros, a former tightrope walker and silent clown, is also a freelance engineer/designer/programmer and sometime performance artist.

1. **Rhode Island's fiscal troubles stem from overindulgence towards unions and poor people**. While personnel costs can't be ignored, the real culprit for our fiscal troubles is the 40-year building spree that sub-urbanized our state. Growing towns could finance services from the growth, which is fine, but only until the growth stops, which it has. Moreover, shrinking older cities saw their property tax bases decline, and when people fled Providence, Woonsocket, Westerly and even Newport, many of the suburbs they found were in another state.

2. **Our current fiscal disaster was the result of forces beyond our control**. Ours is a supply-side failure, due to massive tax cuts over the past 15 years. These include income tax cuts, automobile tax cuts, capital gains tax cuts, and targeted tax cuts and credits for rich people and businesses. In 1990, the state collected a bit more than twice as much in income taxes as in business taxes. In 2008, it was more than triple. In 1997, when asked how the state could afford both of the huge tax cuts the Assembly was considering that year, the fiscal adviser to the House Finance Committee told me, "The chair believes the state would benefit from increased fiscal restraints in the future." Well, here we are.

3. **Our Democrat-dominated legislature means ours is a liberal state**. In an organizational sense, the state Republican party has approximately nothing to offer prospective candidates for state office, and in most towns they have many fewer registered voters than Democrats. Given that, few besides ideologues call themselves Republican. On the other hand, state Democrats are willing to endorse and support anyone who will promise to vote for the current leadership. The result is that Democrats span the ideological spectrum, and much of the real action is in the Democratic primaries.

4. **Labor rules the legislature**. This may have been true once upon a time, but those days are long past. In recent years, labor has lost struggles to retain state employee pension benefits, to retain labor rules for charter schools, and to unionize childcare workers, as well as every high-profile struggle over the state budget. They have negotiated down contracts with the state and most cities and towns, too, accepting healthcare co-pays and reduced cost-of-living increases all over the place.

5. **We are a poor state because of government**. Rhode Island is a poorer state than its neighbors, in part because we are a more urban state than others. But another important reason is in our economic history. The industries that made it big here, like textiles, plastic molding and costume jewelry relied for the most part on unskilled labor, and none of them ever paid the wages of the union-heavy industries of the Midwest. Not only that, but they fled as soon as it was cheaper to make their goods elsewhere. The result is that Rhode Island has one of the most unequal distributions of incomes in the country, and blue-collar work pays less here than the average in our neighboring states, while professional jobs pay about the same.

RENTING

The median monthly rent in Rhode Island in 2007 was $830, and the vacancy rate 7.8 percent. Over 37 percent of renters were paying more than 35 percent of their household income in rent. According to the National Low Income Housing Coalition, an hourly wage of $19.79 is

TAKE 5 FIVE INDUSTRIAL TITANS
OF NINETEENTH CENTURY RHODE ISLAND

1. **George Corliss (1817-1888)**. Corliss patented a new steam engine and founded the Corliss Steam Engine Company in 1856 in Providence. Holder of 68 patents and a notorious control freak, he was an innovator in the areas of mass production and standardization. Corliss provided a steam engine for the Centennial Exposition in Philadelphia in 1876 which supplied juice to 8,000 machines. Corliss refused to let the engine operate on Sundays because of his religious views, and the Exposition was forced to open on Wednesday as a result.

2. **Robert Knight (1826-1912) and Benjamin Knight (1813-1893)**. The Knights were textile kings who established the firm of B.B. & R. Knight Company. At its apex, the Knight empire claimed to be the largest firm in the nation. In the early twentieth century, it owned 19 mills, as well as 15 Rhode Island mill villages. The company, which went under in 1935, developed the "Fruit of the Loom" brand.

3. **William T. Nicholson (1834-1893)**. The Nicholson File Company was founded in 1864 and grew large very fast by gobbling up other file, screw and tool companies, and aggressively courting foreign markets for its products. By the early 1900s, Nicholson had 80 percent of the file market and was producing 120,000 files per day. The company merged with Cooper Industries in 1972, and remains part of Cooper Hand Tools which is headquartered in Raleigh, North Carolina.

needed in Rhode Island in order to secure a two-bedroom apartment without paying more than 30 percent of income for housing costs. Rhode Island ranks among the ten least affordable states in the nation for renters, although within New England, Connecticut and Massachusetts are pricier.

4. **Jabez Gorham (1792-1869)**. Gorham apprenticed and worked with Nehemiah Dodge, a jewelry and silverware pioneer, and then founded his own Providence firm. The business blossomed when Gorham began the manufacture of silver spoons. Gorham's son substantially expanded the business, which included not only the world's largest silverware plant, but also the planet's largest bronze-casting operation. This factory was used to make monuments and statues including the Independent Man atop the Rhode Island Statehouse, and the George Washington monument in the Capitol Rotunda in Washington, DC. Gorham is now headquartered in Bristol, Pennsylvania and is owned by a Kentucky firm.

5. **Samuel P. Colt (1852-1921)**. A nephew of the inventor of the revolver, Colt formed the United States Rubber Company in Providence in 1892. US Rubber produced boots and clothing, and capitalized on the demand for tires in the automobile's early days. The company would go on to be known as Uniroyal, which is now a Michelin brand. In addition to being a rubber titan, Colt served as Attorney General of Rhode Island in the 1880s, and organized the Industrial Trust Company, a leading bank of the day which would later morph into Fleet Bank. Colt was descended on his mother's side from one of Rhode Island's most prominent families, the DeWolfs, and lived at Linden Place in Bristol for many years. Colt left the family farm in Bristol to the state, and it now comprises much of Colt State Park.

1. Lobster
2. Loligo, or long fin squid
3. Scallops
4. Quahogs
5. Fluke

Source: Walter Anoushian, National Marine Fisheries Service, RI & CT Coordinator, and RI Secretary of State.

SELECTED MEDIAN RENTS (2007)

California: $958
Massachusetts: $948
New England: $892
Rhode Island: $830
US: $789
Michigan: $683
Alabama: $601
Iowa: $567

Source: US Census.

LET IT RIDE

Gambling proceeds contribute around $350 million to the state of Rhode Island's budget, accounting for about five percent of state revenues. Gambling revenues come from lottery tickets, Keno sales, dog racing and the state's take from slot machines. Twin River Casino in Lincoln has 4,752 slots, and Newport Grand 1,460. The state has become increasingly dependent on gambling dollars and the 2008 take was $100 million more than that of 2003. However, contrary to previous economic wisdom, gambling is not recession-proof and the state's revenues in this area fell in the second half of 2008 as less money was wagered.

THE GINSU GUYS

The famous Ginsu Knife was the brainchild of Dial Media, a Warwick direct marketing company. Dial was formed in the 1970s by local television ad salesman Ed Valenti and transmission shop owner Barry Becher. The pair, working with Providence ad copywriter Arthur Schiff, took an unexceptional Ohio-made knife, gave it a Japanese-sounding name, and made it a TV sensation. Valenti and Becher were also behind other direct marketing hits including the Miracle Painter and Armourcote Cookware.

The kitschy Ginsu ads featured a karate-inspired intro, and then a demonstration in which the knife was applied to items such as logs, radiator hoses, and tin cans. Following this abuse, the Ginsu would still effortlessly slice a tomato or loaf of bread. The initial offer of the Ginsu (how much would you pay for a knife that can cut through …?) would be followed by the addition of more knives and gadgets (now how much would you pay?), building to a crescendo in which there would be further items (a fruit and vegetable knife that can cut a nail and still go through a pineapple!) and then, unbelievably, still more (but hold on …). Wrapping it all up was a fifty-year guarantee, the promise that the Ginsu was not sold in stores, and a toll free number to call.

In its heyday, Dial Media, which is now among Warren Buffet's stable of companies, was one of the nation's biggest purchasers of spot television time, ranking with Coca-Cola and AT&T. And where are they now? Copywriter Schiff, an advertising legend who wrote 1,800 direct marketing spots for Dial and other companies, died in 2006, and Barry Becher is retired. Ed Valenti is still in the game, however, as co-founder and owner of PriMedia Inc., a media and marketing services company. Valenti also promotes the Ginsu legacy, co-authoring (with Becher) the 2005 book *The Wisdom of Ginsu*. In 2009, a previously unnamed street off Bald Hill Road in Warwick was christened "Ginsu Way." But don't wait, there's no more — there are no current plans to throw in additional Ginsu-named boulevards, overpasses, or city parks.

'25
USA

Slater Mill, 1793

May 29, 1790

Rhode Island

Then and Now

Rhode Island is essential to US Colonial, Revolutionary and industrial history, and is home to a disproportionately large share of sites listed on the National Register of Historic Places. Visitors flock to Providence's Benefit Street, North Kingstown's Wickford Village and Newport for their elegant and well-preserved vistas onto America's past. Yet, for locals, Rhode Island history is as much about the amusement parks, department stores and local celebrities of their youth as it is about historic churches, monuments, or residences. Rhode Islanders will reference a now-vanished drive-in theater or clam shack in the same breath that they point out the site of a shuttered factory, or the scene of a bloody seventeenth century battle between Colonists and Natives. It's a small state, but it's got a lot of stories to tell, both old and new.

POPULATION THEN AND NOW

YEAR	RI (total)	NEW ENGLAND (millions)	USA (millions)
1790	68,825	1.0	3.9
1820	69,122	1.7	9.6
1850	147,545	2.7	23.2
1880	276,531	4.0	50.2
1910	542,610	6.5	92.2

1940	713,346	8.4	132.2
1970	949,723	11.9	203.3
2008	1,050,788	14.3	304.1

Source: US Census Bureau.

RURAL-URBAN POPULATION DIVIDE

	% urban	% rural
1790	19	81
1840	44	56
1910	91	9
1950	87	13
2000	91	9

Source: US Census Bureau.

TURN ON THE LIGHTS

Electricity came to the state in 1882 when the Rhode Island Electric Lighting Company supplied power for lamps in Providence's Market Square. The Rhode Island State House, constructed in the late 1890s, was one of the state's first public buildings to be electrified. The architects, still unsure about the new technology, incorporated plenty of skylights, just in case. National Grid currently supplies all of Rhode Island (except for Burrillville) with electric power, and has 465,000 customers.

They said it

"What cheer, netop?"

– Greeting allegedly extended to Roger Williams by a Narragansett Indian when Williams landed in what is now the Fox Point neighborhood of Providence in 1636. At that time, the water came right up to today's Gano Street, but the area was filled in during the 1820s. Williams landed at "Slate Rock," which was accidentally destroyed by city workers in 1877 when they used dynamite to uncover the historic site where Rhode Island's founder came ashore.

TAKE 5 FIVE MOST POPULOUS RI CITIES AND TOWNS IN 1790
(CURRENT POPULATION IN PARENTHESES)

1. **Newport:** 6,716 (25,359)
2. **Providence:** 6,380 (172,459)
3. **Glocester:** 4,025 (10,536)
4. **South Kingstown:** 4,131 (29,277)
5. **Smithfield:** 3,171 (21,279)

Source: State of Rhode Island Division of Planning, US Census Bureau.

STAY TUNED

Rhode Island's first radio station, WEAN, went on the air in June 1922 and was a promotional vehicle for its owner, Shepard's Department Store. Two months later, the rival Outlet Company launched WJAR. The latter was also Rhode Island's first television station, launched in 1949. For many years, Outlet was both a powerful retailer and a communications company. Outlet the store went bust in 1982, but the media end thrived and was eventually sold to NBC in 1996.

WJAR ("Turn to Ten") has long been the dominant station in the Rhode Island market, often trouncing its competition, particularly for local news. The station boasts such Rhody marquee names as Frank Coletta, Patrice Wood, Jim Taricani and Gene Valicenti, and its alumni include CNN's chief international correspondent, URI grad Christiane Amanpour, as well as Meredith Vieira and Matt Lauer of the *Today Show*. But one name trumps all in the annals of Channel 10 and Rhode Island broadcasting — Art Lake. Lake began his career at WJAR radio in 1944, and five years later became one of the station's original television announcers. He is probably best remembered for his 1963 to 2003 stint as a Channel 10 weatherman, particularly his work with Frank Coletta on the popular *Sunrise* morning show.

TAKE 5 FIVE PIONEERING RHODE ISLAND WOMEN

1. **Anne Hutchinson (1591-1643)**. Hutchinson is considered the first woman to establish an American town. She was born in England and left for Massachusetts in 1634 with her husband William, a prosperous cloth merchant. Like Roger Williams, Hutchinson opposed the rigid Puritan hierarchy she found in her adopted home. Her radical view that religious believers could commune directly with God, without the church as intermediary, resulted in her 1637 arrest and trial for sedition, and then her ejection from the Massachusetts Bay Colony. The Hutchinson family and a group of followers came south and settled in Pocasset (later known as Portsmouth) on the northern tip of Aquidneck Island. William Hutchinson died in 1642 and Anne, fearing the long reach of the Massachusetts authorities, left for Long Island with her unmarried children. This move proved ill-advised, as Hutchinson and all but one of her children were killed by Indians who were engaged in a dispute with Dutch settlers in the area.

2. **Sarah Helen Power Whitman (1803-1878)**. Whitman, an essayist and poet with an interest in transcendentalism, metaphysics and spirituality, was born in Providence and moved to Boston with her husband in 1828. After her husband's 1833 death, she returned to Providence and became a leading writer of the time, as well as a proponent of universal suffrage. In the late 1840s she became engaged to Edgar Allan Poe who had come to Providence to woo her. The two never married.

3. **Elizabeth Buffum Chace (1806-1899)**. Buffum Chace was born in Smithfield and raised as a Quaker. She moved to Fall River, Massachusetts in 1825 and became active in the anti-slavery movement.

Buffum Chace founded the Fall River Anti-Slavery Society with her sisters in 1835, and she and her husband Samuel hid slaves in their home. She returned to Rhode Island and became a founder of the Rhode Island Women's Suffrage Association, as well as an advocate of temperance and prison reform. A mother of 10, Buffum Chace was honored in 2002 with a statue in the Rhode Island State House.

4. **Julia Ward Howe (1819-1910)**. Born in New York City, Howe was descended from a long line of Rhode Island political heavyweights, and spent much of her life in Newport and Portsmouth. A poet and writer, Howe may be most famous for penning "Battle Hymn of the Republic" in 1861, but she was also a well-known advocate for women's suffrage, abolition and prison reform. In 1907, Howe became the first woman elected to the American Academy of Arts and Letters.

5. **Ida Lewis (1842-1911)**. Ida Lewis served as keeper of the Newport Harbor Lime Rock Lighthouse for several decades, and is credited with saving 18 lives, the last when she was 63 years old. Lewis's father was appointed Lime Rock keeper in 1853, but soon suffered a stroke, leaving his wife and eldest daughter Ida to tend the lighthouse. Among Ida's chores as a girl was a daily row to Newport to take her four siblings to school and pick up supplies. Lewis received many visitors at Lime Rock, including President Ulysses S. Grant in 1869.

They said it

THE GREAT DEPRESSION

Even before the Depression began, the local textile industry was showing signs of decline. When the crash came in 1929, things got a lot worse. In the Depression's first two years, 40 percent of textile workers and nearly half of all jewelry industry employees lost their jobs. Moreover, by 1933, wages for industrial workers had plummeted by nearly 50 percent, as had annual retail sales in Providence stores.

Efforts to alleviate the crisis locally came from churches, the Salvation Army and state government, particularly the 1933-1937 administration of Democratic Governor Theodore Francis Green. In

Did you know...

that Ann Franklin (1696-1763) was North America's first female newspaper editor, printer and almanac writer? Franklin and her husband James, who was Benjamin Franklin's brother, founded the colony's first newspaper, the *Rhode Island Gazette* in 1732. The *Gazette* folded after a year and James subsequently died, but Ann went on to produce the *Rhode Island Almanack* and, with her two daughters, print election ballots and other official documents. Moreover, in conjunction with her son, James Jr., Franklin printed colony currency, and established the *Newport Mercury* newspaper in 1758. Her son died in 1762, and Franklin again assumed full control of the family printing and publishing business before her own 1763 death.

Did you know...

that Bristol's annual Fourth of July celebration was inaugurated in 1785, and is the longest running Independence Day parade in the nation?

Washington, the Roosevelt administration sponsored the Works Progress Administration (WPA), among other programs. Rhode Island WPA projects included Goddard Park, Scarborough Beach, East Providence City Hall, Hope and Mount Pleasant High Schools in Providence and Newport's Cliff Walk. Of no less importance were the concerts, plays and murals of the era; these productions put money in the pockets of struggling artists and buoyed the spirits of a downtrodden populace.

The Depression took its toll on public as well as personal finances. By 1939, Providence's debt was over $72 million, and it had to obtain an emergency $2.5 million loan to stave off bankruptcy. As was the case in most parts of the country, recovery didn't come until war time production spurred demand for goods and labor.

Did you know...

that the United States enjoyed a 132-year winning streak in the America's Cup yachting competition? US dominance lasted from the race's 1851 inauguration until a 1983 Australian victory. Newport played host to the famous race between 1930 and 1983, a legacy that is commemorated by America's Cup Avenue which runs through downtown. The winning boats for eight consecutive America's Cup races between 1893 and 1934 were built by the Herreshoff Manufacturing Company (1863-1945) of Bristol. The company's former site is now home to the Herreshoff Marine Museum and America's Cup Hall of Fame.

TAKE 5 MICHAEL BELL'S FIVE QUESTIONS (AND ANSWERS) ABOUT RHODE ISLAND'S VAMPIRE TRADITION

Cranston resident Michael Bell, Ph.D., is an independent public-sector scholar specializing in southern New England folklife. He has served as writer, editor, director and oral historian on numerous studies, articles, programs and projects on topics including Pawtuxet Village, the Looff Carousel, and the occupational folklife of Rhode Island apple orchards and the Narragansett Bay shellfishing industry. Bell frequently lectures before professional, scholarly and popular audiences on the lives and beliefs of everyday Rhode Islanders of both today and generations past. He is the author of the 2001 book *Food for the Dead: On the Trail of New England's Vampires*. A scary sequel is in the works.

1. **Were there actually vampires in Rhode Island?** Absolutely, and not just in Rhode Island. Although Rhode Island has been dubbed "The Transylvania of America," vampires were responsible for an enormous number of deaths throughout New England during the eighteenth and nineteenth centuries. In 1800, one in every 250 people in the Northeast was killed by a vampire, accounting for about one-quarter of all deaths. But this vampire did not resemble the fictional Count Dracula. Indeed, it was so small that it could not be detected with the naked eye, which helps explain why it remained a mysterious killer until 1882, when Robert Koch announced his discovery of the tuberculosis microbe. Rhode Island's vampires, you see, were actually germs.

2. **What did tuberculosis have to do with vampires?** The symptoms of consumption, as pulmonary tuberculosis was then called, correspond closely with vampire folklore. Its victims suffer most at night. They awaken, coughing and in pain, sometimes describing a heavy feeling, like someone sitting on the chest. As the disease progresses, ulcers and cavities develop in the lungs and they begin to cough up blood, which lingers at the corners of the mouth and stains the bedclothes. As they fade into death, others in the family begin to complain of the same symptoms. Unless something is done, all may die. Both consumptives and vampires are the living dead. Consumptives are walking corpses, waiting to die. Pale and wasted, they embody disease and death. Vampires are the incarnation of consumption, an evil that slowly and surreptitiously drains away life.

3. **How did Rhode Islanders kill the vampires?** They exhumed the bodies of deceased relatives and checked them for signs considered to be extraordinary. Liquid blood in the heart was interpreted as "fresh" blood, a sign that the corpse was responsible for the continuing plague of consumption. To stem any further spread of the disease, the heart was cut from the body and burned to ashes. Often it was stipulated that the ashes be fed to any in the family suffering from consumption. A variant of this practice was to burn the entire corpse, sometimes having those afflicted inhale the smoke.

4. **Did Rhode Islanders who dug up their dead relatives refer to them as "vampires"?** In *Food for the Dead*, I concluded that the families involved in this tradition never used the term. But I had to revisit my conclusion with the subsequent discovery of a gravestone in an abandoned cemetery in North Smithfield. Dated 1841, only two ambiguous lines were visible:

Altho' consumption's vampire grasp
Had seized thy mortal frame,

Was the term "vampire" a metaphor, or had the corpses actually been exhumed? Faye Ringel, professor of English at the Coast Guard Academy and a fellow vampire researcher, has shed some light on this epitaph, noting that it is part of a lengthy poem written to commemorate the death of a celebrated abolitionist in 1838. Further lines, buried below concrete, confirmed that the family was plagued by consumption, the metaphorical vampire. We have yet to learn if bodies were exhumed.

5. **Was Nellie Vaughn a vampire?** The legend that Nellie Vaughn, who died in 1889 at the age of 19, was a vampire almost certainly is based on a case of mistaken identity. Students searching for the grave of Mercy Brown of Exeter, who died at the same age in 1892, came upon Nellie's gravestone in West Greenwich. Seeing the inscription "I am waiting and watching for you," they concluded they had found the unnamed vampire their teacher had told them about. Now, Nellie's ghost appears to inform those who visit her gravesite that she is NOT a vampire but is, in her own words, "perfectly pleasant."

WORLD WAR II

The war had a dramatic effect on the state — over 90,000 Rhode Islanders served, and more than 2,500 were killed. Rhode Island also played host to hundreds of thousands of soldiers who trained at the Naval Training Station in Newport, as well as at anti-aircraft and torpedo boat training centers. Naval air bases opened in Westerly and Charlestown, and the Naval Air Station at Quonset Point was the biggest on the East Coast. Torpedoes were produced on Newport's Goat Island, and there were high explosives storage facilities on Gould and Prudence Islands in Narragansett Bay.

The famed "Seabees," seasoned and skilled men employed as the Navy's construction battalion, were stationed at Quonset. During the course of the war they were deployed throughout the globe, and were memorialized in the 1944 John Wayne movie *The Fighting Seabees*.

In addition to the many soldiers from other parts of the US stationed in Rhode Island, the locals were kept busy as moribund factories sprang

TAKE 5 SIX RHODE ISLAND TRAGEDIES

1. **August 12, 1853:** A collision between two trains on the Providence-Worcester Railroad near Pawtucket kills 14.
2. **August 30, 1872:** A Providence-bound steamer, the *Metis*, sinks off Watch Hill after a collision with a schooner, killing over 100 people.
3. **February 11, 1907:** Almost 200 people are killed when the *Larchmont*, a Providence-based steamer, sinks in Block Island Sound after being rammed by another boat in a storm.
4. **May 26, 1954:** Over 100 people die in an explosion and subsequent fire aboard the aircraft carrier USS Bennington, 75 miles off the Rhode Island coast.
5. **December 13, 1977:** A nighttime fire in a women's dorm at Providence College kills 10.
6. **February 20, 2003:** A fire during a concert by the band Great White at the Station Night Club in West Warwick kills 100 and seriously injures many others.

Did you know. . .

that Rhode Island was the only state to reject the Eighteenth Amendment ushering in Prohibition? The Amendment was ratified by most states in 1918 and 1919, but Rhode Island challenged its legality for years. Prohibition's implementation in Rhode Island brought with it an active and sometimes violent bootlegging trade, as well as numerous speakeasies and gin joints.

back to life and new ones were created. The plants made everything from guns to military balloons to the Quonset Hut, a Rhode Island produced prefab shelter extraordinaire. Field's Point on the Cranston-Providence line became a gigantic shipyard; it produced 63 ships in three years, and in 1945 employed over 21,000 people, including 3,000 women.

Rhode Island's large military presence led to it being declared a "vital war zone" in 1942, and added precautions were taken against sabotage and espionage. Approaches to Narragansett Bay were mined to defend against German submarines which had sunk nine merchant ships off the New England coast in the first part of 1942. On May 6, 1945, a day before Germany's surrender, the last Atlantic battle of the war occurred when a German sub which had torpedoed a New York coal ship was sunk by the US Navy just off Block Island.

Did you know. . .

that the Scituate Reservoir, which began operation in 1926 and supplies metro Providence's drinking water, is the result of a 1915 Rhode Island General Assembly vote to flood nearly 15,000 acres of Scituate land? A collection of 1,200 buildings (including hundreds of houses, as well as churches, schools, mills, ice houses, and 30 dairy farms) comprising several mill and farm hamlets were permanently submerged. The Providence and Danielson Railway system was also removed to make way for the reservoir.

SCITUATE, RI, UN HEADQUARTERS

In 1946, Scituate's Chopmist Hill was on the short list of candidates for United Nations headquarters. Chopmist Hill had plenty of open space, easy access to a state airport, and proximity to Boston and New York. Moreover, Chopmist Hill was home to Suddard House, scene of a large and sophisticated WWII radio monitoring system that worked round-the-clock and employed 35-40 operators.

The station, whose function was kept secret from locals, picked up numerous crucial pieces of intelligence during the war, including a report that the Queen Mary carrying 10,000 Allied troops was being targeted for attack. The visiting international delegation tasked with choosing a site also visited the Bristol/Portsmouth area, but despite the best efforts of then Governor John O. Pastore and other officials, Rhode Island lost out to New York in the UN derby.

TAKE 5 FIVE AUTOMOTIVE FIRSTS

1. **First car in Rhode Island (1896).** The steam-powered model was produced by the A.T. Cross Company of writing implement fame.
2. **First automobile race on a track in the US (1896).** The event was held in Cranston at Narragansett Trotting Park, currently Cranston Stadium. The winner completed the five-mile race in just over 15 minutes. A banked and paved surface for the track debuted in 1915.
3. **First automobile parade in the US is held in Newport (1899).**
4. **First Rhode Island license plate issued (1904).** A Wakefield doctor scores the ultimate coup — the number one plate. Rhode Island had 767 registered cars in 1904, and by 1921 there were over 43,000. The state now has more than 800,000 motor vehicles registered to ndividuals, businesses and government entities.
5. **First jail sentence for speeding (1904).** A Newport judge busts a driver traveling 20 mph. It was the lead-foot's second offence.

PUBLIC TRANSPORTATION

The Rhode Island Public Transit Authority (RIPTA) carried over 25 million passengers in fiscal year 2008. This figure might sound impressive, but Rhode Island transit ridership hit 154 million in 1923 despite a much smaller population, and was also over 150 million in 1944 when war-time gas rationing garaged many cars. RIPTA, which was established in 1966, is a quasi public independent authority established to provide transportation throughout the state.

Public transportation debuted in Rhode Island in 1864 when 10 horse-drawn cars traveled on rails between Providence's Market Square and Main Street in Pawtucket. The 4.5 mile trip took 45 minutes and cost 10 cents. In the years following, service expanded rapidly and many companies arose to compete for the rider's dime. The city of Providence was enjoying explosive growth at its fringes, and the horse-drawn cars were both cause and effect of this expansion.

Electrification came in the late 1880s, and service by this time extended to Woonsocket, Cranston, Warwick and the cities of the East Bay. In the early 1900s, Providence was thick with all manner of trolleys and trams heading up College Hill, to nearby suburbs like Silver Lake and Elmwood, and to farther-flung destinations including Scituate and the Crescent Park and Rocky Point amusement parks.

The advent of paved roads and gas-powered vehicles produced the trolley's decline, and by the mid-1950s they had been replaced by buses. In the post-WWII era, the movement of people and jobs away from central cities, as well as the construction of highways, has made the private automobile the dominant mode of transportation.

Did you know...

that T.F. Green Airport, originally called Hillsgrove State Airport, opened in 1933? The airport site was dedicated in 1931 with two air shows that attracted 150,000 people, over 20 percent of the state's population of the time.

WALTER "SALTY" BRINE (1918-2004)

One would be hard pressed to find a more beloved Rhode Islander than broadcaster Salty Brine. Brine started at WPRO radio in 1942, and was on the air for more than 50 years. He also hosted, with his collie Jeff, the live kids' television program *Salty Brine's Shack* which ran from 1955 to 1968. Salty's seaside shanty became so embedded in local lore that some believed it was an actual place, rather than a set created for a TV show.

Brine's trademark skipper's hat, his artificial leg (the result of a boyhood accident with a train) and his warm manner endeared him to

TAKE 5 FIVE DEPARTED RHODE ISLAND DEPARTMENT STORES

1. **Shepard's**. Shepard's was founded in 1880 and became the largest department store in New England. The store's exterior clock on Westminster Street in downtown Providence was a landmark, and its Tea Room a popular spot for lunch. The flagship store, which closed in 1974, once anchored downtown Providence's shopping district; now it houses the University of Rhode Island's Extension Division.

2. **The Outlet Company**. A competitor to Shepard's, the Outlet opened in 1891 on Weybosset Street. It closed in 1982 and its downtown building burned down in 1986; the site is now occupied by Johnson & Wales University.

3. **Gladding's**. The store had its origins in a 1766 dry goods store, and moved to Westminster Street in downtown Providence in 1891. The company was sold in 1972.

4. **Peerless**. Another Westminster Street department store, Peerless operated stores throughout the state until its closing in 1991. The original Peerless Building is now home to upscale lofts, and previously housed Lupo's nightclub.

5. **Ann & Hope**. A discount pioneer, Ann & Hope opened in an old Cumberland Mill in 1953. It ceased operations as a full-fledged department store in 2001, but still operates Garden Outlets and Curtain and Bath Outlets, including stores in Warwick and Cumberland.

Did you know. . .

that Bradley Hospital in East Providence was the first psychiatric hospital for children in the US? It opened in 1931, and commemorates Emma Pendleton Bradley, who was born in 1879. As a seven-year-old, Emma contracted encephalitis, which resulted in epilepsy, cerebral palsy and mental retardation. At the time, there were no hospitals for mentally ill children, and so Emma was cared for at home. She ultimately died at age 27 in 1907, and her parents left their estate to the establishment of a hospital for children with psychiatric problems.

multiple generations of Rhode Islanders. He had several signature catchphrases, notably, "Brush your teeth and say your prayers" at sign-off time, and "No school Foster-Glocester," which he would pronounce with great gusto when listing school closures due to snow. Recognizing Brine's status as local icon, the state of Rhode Island named a piece of the Narragansett shore in his honor in 1990, and one can now swim at "Salty Brine State Beach."

Brine was elected to the Rhode Island Heritage Hall of Fame in 1979, and the inaugural class of the Rhode Island Radio Hall of Fame in 2008. Salty's son, Wally Brine, is himself a radio veteran and one half of the long running *Loren & Wally Morning Show* on WROR in Boston.

Did you know. . .

that in 1924, the Ku Klux Klan attracted 8,000 people to a rally in Foster? Throughout the 1920s, the Klan was popular in northwestern Rhode Island where it would hold clambakes and oyster dinners. Its members held local offices, and the police chiefs of several Rhode Island cities were Klan members. The Klan's enmity was not limited to Blacks, but also included Jews, Catholics and immigrants.

TAKE 5 JIM TARICANI'S TOP FIVE
STORIES HE HAS COVERED

Jim Taricani is an investigative reporter on behalf of WJAR NBC 10 in Providence. Taricani has worked in Rhode Island print, radio and television journalism since the early 1970s, specializing in crime and government corruption issues. The youngest person to be inducted into the Rhode Island Heritage Hall of fame, Taricani has won numerous awards for his work including an Edward R. Murrow award for investigative journalism, and a 2005 Press Freedom award from the Reporters' Committee for Freedom of the Press. In 2004, Taricani was sentenced to six months of home confinement by a federal judge for failing to disclose a confidential source who leaked a tape related to the FBI's "Operation Plunder Dome" investigation into corruption at Providence City Hall. Taricani has given numerous interviews, speeches and lectures on First Amendment issues, and has been a strong advocate for a law shielding journalists from divulging confidential sources.

1. **The Patriarca Crime Family**. I began covering the Patriarca crime family in the mid-1970s. Over time, with a lot of help from law enforcement experts and my own surveillance and investigative work, I developed a good working knowledge of this mafia family that controlled the rackets in New England. At one time, I was preparing a book on the life of one of Raymond Patriarca's hit men — Nicky Palmigiano. When the namesake of the family died in the early 80s, his son, Raymond "J" Patriarca, invited me to his father's wake. He wanted to make sure I had an accurate picture for my book of all the people who paid homage to his father. I still cover the "mob," but it's not what it used to be, thanks to the efforts of Rhode Island State Police, the Providence Police and the FBI.

2. **State Government in Rhode Island**. I have been covering politics and government for most of my 35-year career. It never ceases to amaze me how parochial, out-dated and impractical our state government seems to be. With one party — the Democrats — dominating the state legislature

for the past 50 years, it makes it difficult, at best, for any meaningful reform. So many of our state leaders seem more concerned about maintaining their power base than legislating for the people. And the history of government corruption over the years is simply sad.

3. **Retrial of Claus von Bulow**. I worked this trial to the bone. I got to know von Bulow and his girlfriend Andrea Reynolds quite well. They thought I was a straightforward reporter and I was invited to interview von Bulow in his ex-wife Sunny's apartment in New York City on two occasions. After he was acquitted, he granted me the first extended interview. He was a fascinating man, full of mystery, and himself. He didn't testify during the trial, so in my exclusive interview with him I asked, "Did you try to kill your wife, Sunny?"
He looked at me with cold eyes, took a drag on his ever-present cigarette, and answered smoothly, "I was found not guilty, wasn't I?"

4. **The Sex Trade in Rhode Island, Particularly in Providence.** Lawmakers refuse to close a loophole in Rhode Island's prostitution law, which makes prostitution legal as long as it takes place between adults behind closed doors. Young Asian women are enslaved into working in dozens of "massage parlors" in Providence, which are nothing but brothels. It is simply ridiculous for our legislators to refuse to do anything about this. Makes me wonder where some of them get their massages.

5. **Toxic Waste Dumping**. My original producer Gary Scurka and I uncovered a scheme involving mob-backed "carting companies." These were New Jersey-based garbage companies that were dumping toxic waste from Garden State chemical plants in our state landfill. We aired this half-hour special in 1980, and it resulted in state and federal investigations, along with many of the New Jersey chemical companies paying major fines to Rhode Island to help clean up the toxic mess.

AMUSEMENT PARKS

The late 1800s was a time of rapid urbanization, modernization and industrialization. Densely packed city dwellers sought ways to blow off steam, whether at the beach, in newly created urban oases like Roger Williams Park, or at amusement parks. These attractions were a trolley ride away for city folk, making them easy and popular day trips. In the post-WWII era, amusement parks remained popular, but by the 1970s their appeal had begun to wane.

- **Vanity Fair, East Providence (1907-1912).** Vanity Fair was a spectacular venue which featured a 1.6 million gallon pool as well as a railway, ballroom, and vaudeville theatre. There were also animal shows and exotic entertainments including Wild West and Japanese themed villages. A crowd pleaser was the "Fighting the Flames" show in which firemen rescued people from burning buildings. The park had financial troubles from the outset, and was struck by a real fire which resulted in its 1912 closure. In 1915 Standard Oil bought the land to use for oil storage, and it is currently the site of Silver Spring Golf Course.

- **Crescent Park, Riverside (1886-1979).** Crescent Park was developed in the mid-1880s and was inspired by Coney Island. It is most famous today for its 1895 carousel, which was designed by Charles Looff, a master Danish carver. The Crescent Park Carousel is still in operation, and is the only piece of the park that was saved. It

TAKE5 TOP FIVE RHODE ISLAND
BABY GIRLS' NAMES

	1960	2007
1.	Donna	Sophia
2.	Susan	Ava
3.	Mary	Isabella
4.	Linda	Madison
5.	Karen	Olivia

None of the five most popular 2007 girls' names appeared in 1960's top 100.

Source: Social Security Administration.

appears on the National Register of Historic Places, and was also named Rhode Island's State Symbol of Folk Art.

- **Rocky Point, Warwick (1847-1996)**. In its early days, Rocky Point was a sleepy place for church picnics, but by the early 1900s, it was a southern New England hot spot packed with rides, attractions and shows. Over the years, it also played host to big name concerts and major political rallies. Rocky Point's "Shore Dinner Hall" was reputedly the world's largest, and the park was the site of the first presidential phone call, an 1877 chat between Rutherford B. Hayes and Alexander Graham Bell, stationed 10 miles up the road in Providence.

Did you know...

that the 165,000 square foot Cranston Street Armory in Providence's West Broadway neighborhood not only served as home to the Rhode Island National Guard, it also hosted track meets, auto shows, boxing matches, circuses, inaugural balls and political rallies? Known as "the Castle," the Medieval Gothic style Armory has 90-foot ceilings and was built in 1907. The Armory is now largely vacant, and preservationists are concerned that the yellow brick behemoth will fall into complete disrepair if efforts aren't taken to restore it. Proposals to use the Armory as a movie sound stage or as a home for the state's archives have so far not borne fruit.

Crime and Punishment

The Ocean State's mob legacy, its history of official corruption, and some highly publicized murders have produced an association in the minds of many between "crime" and "Rhode Island." Despite this image, Rhode Island is quite safe, with the exception of some high crime spots in the state's poorer urban areas. Rhode Island not only has less violent crime on average than the US as a whole, it has a lower violent crime rate than the New England region. But do go ahead and secure your vehicle — Rhode Island's property crime rate is higher than that of the Northeast or New England.

Statistics notwithstanding, Rhode Island does have some exceptional crime lore, with a cast of characters that includes swindling bankers, graft-taking politicians, and Mafia kingpins, not to mention your garden variety murderers and thugs.

RATING RHODE ISLAND CRIME

- Rhode Island violent crime rate: 227 per 100,000
- New England violent crime rate: 304
- US violent crime rate: 467
- Rhode Island property crime rate: 2,623 per 100,000
- New England property crime rate: 2,365
- US property crime rate: 3,263

1. **Destruction/damage/vandalism**: 12,839
2. **Assault** (includes simple, aggravated, intimidation): 10,924
3. **Larceny theft** (includes shoplifting, theft of affixed motor vehicle parts, theft from motor vehicles and buildings as well as purse snatching, pick pocketing and all other forms): 19,068
4. **Burglary/breaking and entering**: 5,161
5. **Drugs/narcotics violations**: 4,696

Source: Rhode Island State Police (2007).

- Year in RI with highest violent crime rate: 1981*
- Year in RI with highest property crime rate: 1980*
- Year in RI with highest rate of vehicle theft: 1975*

Stats are post 1960. Source: FBI.

RHODE ISLAND'S LAST EXECUTION

Rhode Island's final execution took place in 1845 when Irish immigrant John Gordon was hanged for the murder of textile baron Amasa Sprague, a member of one of Rhode Island's wealthiest and most influential families. John Gordon's brother, Nicholas, ran a store-cum-tavern near the Sprague factory in Cranston, and this displeased Sprague who did not like his workers whiling away their lunch hours drinking. He used his influence to have Gordon's liquor license revoked. When Sprague's bludgeoned dead body was found in the snow on New Year's Eve 1843, Nicholas Gordon and his brothers John and William became suspects and were tried for the crime.

The trial pitted the power of the dominant Yankee aristocracy against a rising population of pro-labor immigrant Catholics from Ireland. The trial was infused with anti-Irish sentiment, and there was notable bias on the part of both the judge and the jury. William

They said it

"I was convicted of being the mayor."
– Buddy Cianci in the wake of his conviction on a RICO conspiracy charge in 2002 as part of Operation Plunder Dome. Cianci had been acquitted of specific crimes, but his apparent knowledge of a criminal enterprise at City Hall, and his association with criminal conspirators, allowed the government to bring a criminal conspiracy charge against him.

Gordon was acquitted and Nicholas freed due to a hung jury, but John Gordon was convicted and hanged, a result that was widely seen as a miscarriage of justice.

The General Assembly abolished capital punishment in 1852, although in 1872 it was reinstated for murders committed while under life imprisonment. In 1984, capital punishment was removed from state law, regardless of circumstances.

NUMBER OF CRIMES YEARLY
- 18 murders
- 223 arson
- 3,205 motor vehicle thefts
- 253 forced rape
- 37 kidnapping, abduction
- 759 weapon law violations
- 16 extortion/blackmail
- 2 bribery
- 48 pornography/obscene material
- 93 fraud — impersonation

Source: Rhode Island State Police (2007).

Raymond Patriarca (1908-1984) and the New England Mob

Raymond L.S. Patriarca, whose base was the Federal Hill neighborhood of Providence, presided over the New England Mafia for several decades. Patriarca was a well known figure on the Hill, and sometimes surveyed his domain from an Atwells Avenue sidewalk lawn chair. Officially, his livelihood was vending machines, but Patriarca's real business was controlling networks of gambling, prostitution, extortion, loan sharking and high level larceny. His reach extended throughout New England and as far south as New York City, where he sometimes would meet with members of the New York Mafia's "five families." Patriarca and his associates infiltrated and exerted influence on labor unions, government, the police, banks, and even the judiciary.

The Worcester, Massachusetts-born Patriarca came to Providence as a toddler, and got started in crime early on. He was first arrested as a teenager, and repeatedly thereafter for everything from armed robbery, to accessory to jail break, lewd cohabitation, conspiracy to commit murder, and racketeering. Law enforcement was well aware of at least some of Patriarca's illicit activities, and he was on their radar from the 1930s until his 1984 death of natural causes at his girlfriend's North Providence home.

Numerous bugs and surveillance tapes, as well as the testimony of fellow mobsters seeking to avoid prison or have their sentences reduced, established that Patriarca was the New England boss of *La Cosa Nostra*. Patriarca repeatedly denied this claim, railing against law enforcement and the media, notably the *Providence Journal*, for defaming him. Unlike a number of real life and fictional gangsters, Patriarca avoided mobster flash, living modestly on Federal Hill, and in his later years, in suburban Johnston.

Despite the romance associated with the mob, gangsters are a grisly bunch, and none more so than the boss himself who was twice convicted of conspiracy to commit murder. Moreover, it was only Patriarca's failing health while in his 70s that kept him from being tried for his role in two other murders. At the time of his 1984 death, Patriarca was also under indictment on federal racketeering charges, but was deemed too ill to travel to Florida to face trial.

Patriarca's passing closed a chapter in local mob history, and in its wake there was a power struggle in which Patriarca's son, Raymond Jr., was unable to exert the level of control over the "family" as had his father. Two of Jr.'s close associates, Billy "The Wild Guy" Grasso, and Francis "Cadillac Frank" Salemme, were shot in 1989, Grasso fatally.

Patriarca Jr. wound up serving time for racketeering in the 1990s and left the organized crime business, although he remains in the area. The reputed boss of the local mob since the mid-1990s is Luigi Giovanni "Baby Shanks" Manocchio, an octogenarian with a lengthy criminal past who took over the reins from Salemme.

Regardless of the configuration of the players, the Mafia's influence in Rhode Island has waned substantially in the last 25 years. The Racketeer Influenced and Corrupt Organizations Act, or RICO, which debuted in 1970 as a means to capture mob bosses, changed the organized crime landscape and made it much harder for leaders to insulate themselves from crimes committed by street level enforcers. Organized crime is still extant in the state, however, as evidenced by the dozens of crooks picked up in "Operation Mobbed Up" in November 2008, and the 30 arrests made in a multi-agency organized crime bust in February 2009.

They said it

"In this thing of ours, your love for your mother and father is one thing; your love for The Family is a different kind of love."
— **Rhode Island mob boss Raymond L.S. Patriarca in comments recorded while under electronic surveillance.**

FINE, THEN

- Speeding: $85 (1-10 mph over limit); $195 for 11 mph over limit, plus $10 for each additional mph
- Red light violation: $75
- Eluding a traffic light (e.g., cutting through a parking lot to avoid a light): $75
- Failure to wear a seatbelt: $75
- Expired registration or license: $75
- Littering: Up to $500
- Driving without proof of liability insurance: $500
- Failing to stop for a school bus with flashing red lights: Up to $300 and/or license suspension for up to 30 days

Source: Rhode Island DMV.

CELEBRITY MISDEEDS

Long before he was Michael Corleone or Tony Montana, and certainly before he smelled the scent of a woman, a 21-year-old Al Pacino was arrested in 1961 in Woonsocket for carrying a concealed weapon. Another star nabbed by Rhode Island's finest was Mick Jagger, who got no satisfaction on a July 1972 evening when foggy weather forced the Stones to land at T.F. Green Airport in Warwick instead of Boston, where they were to perform a concert. A *Providence Journal* photographer attempted an impromptu photo session with rock and roll's bad boys, but Jagger objected and assaulted the shutterbug, resulting in Mick's arrest.

On a more positive note, in June 2008 Bill Cosby visited the Adult Correctional Institute (ACI) in Cranston. Cosby, sporting a

Community College of Rhode Island athletics T-shirt, delivered an inspirational talk to ACI graduates in which he implored them to believe in themselves and take responsibility for their actions.

UNDER THE INFLUENCE

Under Rhode Island law, motor vehicle operators who register a blood alcohol level (BAC) over 0.08 are charged with driving while intoxicated (DWI). For those 21 years and younger, a BAC between 0.02 and 0.08 is sufficient to produce a driving under the influence (DUI) charge.

It is not possible to refuse a chemical test in Rhode Island without penalty — refusal to take a breathalyzer test results in a six-month license suspension, as well as fines and community service. There are varying penalties for DWI in Rhode Island depending on the age of the driver, previous offenses and BAC level — a BAC over 0.15 triggers greater sanctions.

The highest BAC recorded in the state occurred in July 2008 when Stanley Kobierowski of North Providence was arrested after crashing into a message board on I-95 near Providence Place Mall. Kobierowski's BAC was 0.491, over time six times the legal limit, and a level that often produces death or at least unconsciousness. Kobierowski was placed in a detox unit and sedated prior to being arraigned.

Did you know. . .

that in 2008, Providence was ranked 213 worst out of 385 US cities in crime rate (murder, rape, robbery, aggravated assault, burglary and motor vehicle theft)? Ramapo, New York, a city of 114,000 located 30 miles northwest of New York City, had the lowest crime rate in the nation, while New Orleans had the worst. Other New England rankings: Boston, MA, 286; Worcester, MA, 222; New Bedford, MA, 250; Bridgeport, CT, 326; Hartford, CT, 359.

TAKE 5   ZACHARY MALINOWSKI'S FIVE
NOTABLE RHODE ISLAND MOB HITS

Investigative reporter W. Zachary Malinowski has been working for the *Providence Journal* since 1985. He specializes in stories on crime, government corruption, and the judicial system, and has covered everything from criminal gangs, to the Operation Plunder Dome investigation to the state of the New England Mafia.

1. **July 13, 1966: At the behest of New England Mob boss Raymond Patriarca, hit man Joseph Barboza Baron shoots and kills Willie Marfeo at a Federal Hill phone booth**. Marfeo had gotten on Patriarca's bad side by running an unauthorized dice game. Baron was jailed for Marfeo's murder, but testified against Patriarca, and the latter was sent to federal prison in Atlanta. While in jail, Patriarca received a 10-year sentence in Rhode Island for conspiring to kill Marfeo's brother and another man who were shot in a Providence grocery store in 1968. Hit man Barboza Baron, aka "Joe the Baron," was relocated to California under the Federal Witness Protection Program, but was gunned down in San Francisco in 1975.

2. **April 3, 1978: Joseph P. "Joe Onions" Scanlon is gunned down in a social club on Knight Street on Federal Hill in Providence**. The club's owner, Andrew F. Merola, and another man, Nicholas Pari, both known mob associates, were charged with Scanlon's murder. This is a notable mob hit because Merola and Pari were the first two suspects in the history of the state to be found guilty of murder without the victim's body as evidence. They appealed their convictions and later pleaded guilty to lesser murder-related charges. The body remained missing for 30 years until November 19, 2008 when Scanlon's remains were found buried 14 feet deep in a grassy area behind an apartment complex in the Riverside section of East Providence. Pari, confined to a wheelchair and dying of cancer, told the state police where Scanlon had been buried.

3. **September 22, 1982: Raymond "Slick" Vecchio, a two-bit Federal Hill punk with an extensive criminal record, is murdered while having a few drinks at Vincent's on the Hill.** As patrons looked on, two men wearing ski masks burst into the restaurant and fired five shots. Three bullets hit Vecchio in the head. Another struck him the chest. Vecchio fell to the floor dead. No one was ever charged in connection with the murder, but the police always suspected that one of the killers was Kevin T. Hanrahan, a known muscle guy for the mob.

4. **September 23, 1992: A decade and one day after Vecchio's hit, Kevin T. Hanrahan, one of the suspected killers, is killed.** Hanrahan was ambushed just after finishing a meal at the Arch Restaurant on Atwells Avenue on Federal Hill, just down the street from where Vecchio was murdered. Two men stepped in front of him and pumped three slugs into his head. No one has ever been arrested for the killing of Hanrahan, a known shakedown artist, enforcer and drug dealer.

5. **May 8, 1994: Barry R. Kourmpates, a small-time thief from Cranston who had just been released from the Adult Correctional Institutions, is executed near the lighthouse at Beavertail State Park Point in Jamestown.** He was shot several times and the body set on fire. The Rhode Island mob wanted Kourmpates snuffed out because he was involved in a burglary ring that stole hundreds of thousands of dollars in cash and jewels from safes in places such as East Greenwich. The problem was that Kourmpates and his pals broke into the homes of several people with mob connections. They were told to return the booty, but Kourmpates told them to get lost. The murder remains unsolved.

Claus Von Bulow

It was the ultimate pre-O.J. celebrity trial — a dashing and cultured European gentleman is accused of killing his wife, heir to a fortune worth over $75 million. The scene of the crime: Clarendon Court, a lavish 23-room Newport mansion set on 10 waterfront acres.

The prosecution charged that Danish-born Claus von Bulow, who had tried to murder his wife, Sunny, in 1979 by injecting her with insulin, made a second attempt in 1980, this time causing her to lapse into a coma from which she never emerged. The motive was clear — von Bulow was having an affair with a soap opera actress and wished to dispense with his wife and get his hands on her estate. The defense countered by suggesting that Sunny's coma was self-inflicted, and that she was a flighty, depressed woman addled by drug and drink.

It was Sunny's second marriage; previously she had been married to an Austrian prince, Alfie von Auersperg, from whom she was divorced in 1965. Coincidentally, the Prince also lapsed into an irreversible coma, his following a 1983 car crash.

The first chapter of the von Bulow affair wound up on March 16, 1982. Claus was convicted of two counts of attempted murder following a five-week Newport trial in which the state called 56 witnesses. The verdict was immediately appealed, and von Bulow freed on bail. The case was retried in Providence in 1985, and this time von Bulow was acquitted. Sunny's two children by her first marriage then filed a $56 million civil suit against von Bulow, which was settled when he agreed to divorce their comatose mother and relinquish any claim to her fortune. The daughter that Claus and Sunny had had together remained loyal to her father in the proceedings.

The von Bulow case set the table for later celebrity trials — the second trial was one of the first fully-televised such events, and Dominick Dunne covered it blow by blow for *Vanity Fair*. Alan Dershowitz led von Bulow's appeal, and subsequently wrote a book about it called *Reversal of Fortune*, later made into an eponymous movie starring Glenn Close and Jeremy Irons.

Sunny Bulow never awoke from her coma and died in a New York City nursing home in December 2008. In the wake of the trials, Claus returned to Europe and now lives in London where he writes book reviews and continues to attend society functions.

THE BIG HOUSE

- Total number of Rhode Island prisoners: About 3,700
- Percentage of Rhode Island prisoners who are women: About 6
- Total number of Rhode Island prisoners in 1976: About 600
- Number of people employed by the Department of Corrections: About 1,500
- Percentage of inmates serving six months or less: 61
- Rhode Island's rank among US states in probationers per 100,000 adult residents: 5
- Odds a Pawtucket or Providence man between the ages of 25-29 is on probation or parole: 1 in 7
- Number of prisoners serving a life sentence as of 12/31/07: 165 (23 are serving out of state, and 27 are serving life without parole)
- Percentage of sentenced inmates who return within 24 months of release: 46

Source: Rhode Island Department of Corrections (2008).

IN THE LINE OF DUTY

Forty-four Rhode Island law enforcement officials have been killed in the line of duty; this total includes accidental deaths, as well as loss of life from gunfire and assault. The agencies with the most deaths are the Providence PD with eight officers killed, followed by the Rhode Island State Police with seven and the Warwick PD with five.

One of the more shocking recent police deaths was the 2005 killing of Providence Police Detective Sergeant James Allen. Allen was shot with his own weapon inside Providence Police Department (PPD)

Did you know. . .

that it is not permitted to park overnight on city streets in Providence and Cranston? Cars parked during the wee hours are ticketed, and some people, particularly owners of duplexes, have paved over pieces of lawn to create parking spaces.

Headquarters by Esteban Carpio, a young man being questioned in connection with the stabbing of an 84-year-old woman. Carpio jumped from a window following the shooting, but was soon apprehended by PPD officers. At trial, Carpio's defense argued that he was

Fugitive Banker: Joseph Mollicone

Bank president Joseph Mollicone didn't just embezzle $13 million, he precipitated a banking crisis that left thousands of Rhode Islanders without access to their money, some for as long as a year and a half. The banking crisis also served to intensify an early 1990s recession already battering Rhode Island.

Mollicone headed Heritage Loan and Investment Company, which he looted for personal gain. He was accused of making phony loans, as well as providing services to organized crime figures. Mollicone's late father, also a banker, had had a relationship with Raymond Patriarca, whose headquarters were a short walk from the elder Mollicone's office.

Joseph Mollicone was a high flyer who, while president of Heritage Loan, was also involved in dozens of businesses, land deals and other ventures. More importantly, he was vice chair of the Rhode Island Share and Deposit Indemnity Corporation (RISDIC), which insured the state's banks. The cozy relationship between Heritage and the RISDIC proved costly, and ultimately the RISDIC was declared insolvent, throwing Rhode Island's banks into crisis.

The revelations of corruption at Heritage and the RISDIC came in the fall of 1990, shortly before an election that pitted incumbent Governor Edward DiPrete against challenger Bruce Sundlun (who won the contest). DiPrete was accused of lax oversight of the state's banks,

psychotic; however, he was convicted of Allen's murder as well as the stabbing that had brought him to the police station in the first place. While no one disputed that Carpio had killed Allen, the PPD was assailed by some for failing to recognize that Carpio was mentally ill,

and was linked to Mollicone by way of sweetheart leases negotiated between DiPrete associates and Mollicone. The busy banker also had ties to Providence Mayor Buddy Cianci, whose home he purchased. Cianci later returned the favor by buying condo units from Mollicone, borrowing the money, naturally, from Heritage Loan.

Mollicone was confronted by authorities with the irregularities in his bank on November 1, 1990; a week later he disappeared. On January 1, 1991, his first day in office, Governor Bruce Sundlun closed Rhode Island's banks and credit unions. More than a billion dollars of depositor money was frozen, and some of the institutions did not reopen.

For his part, Mollicone went underground, calling himself John Fazioli and settling in Salt Lake City. He moved in with a woman, and came up with his share of the rent by getting cash advances on a credit card that the girlfriend obtained for him. Mollicone returned to Rhode Island in 1992 and surrendered. In 1993, he was convicted of embezzlement, bank fraud and conspiracy. He ended up serving 10 years of a 30-year sentence, and was also assessed $420,000 in fines and $12 million in restitution. The onetime banking mogul, who now lives in Warwick, has been paying $2,500 annually on his debt (10 percent of his $25,000 salary working for a Providence metal stamping company).

and for repeatedly punching him in the face when they caught him after the shooting.

Prior to Allen's death, the last officer death in Providence was the controversial shooting of 29-year-old Providence Police Department Sergeant Cornel Young Jr. outside a Providence restaurant. The African American Young, whose father is retired PPD Major Cornel Young Sr.,

TAKE 5 ARLENE VIOLET'S TOP FIVE
MEMORABLE MOMENTS AS ATTORNEY GENERAL

Arlene Violet grew up in Providence and Cranston and is a former member of the Sisters of Mercy religious order. While still a nun, Violet earned a law degree, and ultimately was elected Rhode Island Attorney General, becoming the United States' first woman to hold that post. She served as Rhode Island Attorney General from 1985 to 1987, and then went on to a successful career on local talk radio, broadcasting her last show in December 2006. Violet is currently a practicing attorney, writes a column for the *Valley Breeze* newspaper, and is a weekly news analyst on the WPRI Channel 12 Newsmakers program.

1. One mob informant with whom I was meeting launched into a recitation about how he had found God, and was a changed man and so his sentence should be drastically reduced. "Let's be perfectly clear about you," I said as I stared at him with a look that would pierce cement. "You are a murderer and robber. I don't particularly like you, or what you represent. I want you to cooperate, but it will be on my terms."
He blurted out, "And I thought you were a Sister of Mercy!"
2. When I was running for Attorney General, a caller to a talk show where I was a guest opined, "Politics is a dirty business for a woman, let alone a nun. Why do you want to dirty yourself?"
"Precisely," I responded.

was off-duty and was trying to break up a fight when other members of the Providence PD arrived on the scene. Young had his weapon drawn, and the officers mistook him for a suspect and opened fire, killing him.

In the aftermath of the shooting, the department noted that Young had not identified himself as an officer or shown his badge, and that when the patrolmen demanded that he drop his gun, Young failed to do so. The

"Huh?" the man asked.

"That's precisely why I am running. Women have to deal with dirty laundry all the time."

3. I attended monthly meetings with Rhode Island police chiefs, all men. It took them a while to get used to me being there. After the third meeting, the Cumberland police chief kissed me goodbye, but then caught himself, and said to the raucous laughter of his colleagues, "I never kissed an attorney general before!"

"Let's hope not," I responded.

4. It is rarely good news when 60 Minutes comes to town to do a story. Morley Safer was my interviewer. After several hours, he asked, "Five years ago, you prayed for an hour each day. Fine for a lawyer, fine for a nun. What about as Attorney General?"

"You wouldn't believe all the prayers I said before you came to town," I quipped.

5. A national newspaper came to cover the first of four meetings of all the United States Attorneys General. The reporter asked me, "What's the best thing about being the only woman among the 50?"

"That's easy," I replied, "There's never a line at the ladies room!"

officers were not charged criminally for the death, and the department portrayed the shooting as a tragic accident. Others, including the slain officer's mother, Leisa Young, weren't so sure. Many felt that the outcome would have been different if Young had been Caucasian, and that the officers and the PPD bore responsibility for what was a racially biased incident. Leisa Young brought a $20 million wrongful death suit against the department, alleging that its inadequate training and policies concerning off-duty officers had contributed to her son's death. One of the prosecutions lawyers was Innocence Project founder Barry Scheck, a member of O.J. Simpson's criminal defense team. Scheck was removed from the case, and Judge Mary M. Lisi eventually threw out the suit.

Plunder Dome and Beyond

Operation Plunder Dome was the name of the federal investigation into corruption at Providence City Hall in the 1990s. The government's detailed case against then-mayor Buddy Cianci and his co-conspirators argued that Providence was "a city for sale," and that City Hall was run as a criminal enterprise in which kickbacks, bribes, and forced campaign contributions were routine.

These revelations did not come as a shock to Rhode Islanders; after all, during Cianci's early 1980s regime a number of city officials, including Highway Superintendant Edward "Buckles" Melise, were also jailed. The locus of 1980s corruption was the public works department where paving materials were stolen for use on outside contracts, kickbacks demanded on the sale of city garbage trucks and private snowplow operators extorted. There were also no-show jobs, phony overtime claims and mob connections to the city's administration, notably that of Patriarca crime family member Frank L. "Bobo" Marrapese, and Public Works Department employee William "Black Jack" Del Santo.

In the 1990s, the Feds' investigation focused on the tax department. The key witness in the Plunder Dome trial was businessman Antonio Freitas who secretly recorded over 150 conversations with city officials in 1998 and 1999. Freitas, who had initially gone to the government when

PIRATES AND PRIVATEERS

Piracy and privateering were rampant in Rhode Island in the 1700s. Piracy, despite its colorful connection with parrots, planks and eye-patches, is armed robbery at sea, while privateering involves giving privately owned ships authority to attack enemy owned vessels, bring them into port, and seize their goods. Privateering in Colonial days worked both ways — sometimes Rhode Islanders were doing the seizing, and other times they were on the receiving end. In 1689, Block Island was captured and looted by French privateers, and Colony soldiers were dispatched from Newport to repel the invaders. The French fled following a two-hour battle, and their commander was

he felt he unfairly lost out on a bid to lease property to the city, was part of a sting operation in which he passed bribes to city officials in exchange for tax favors and city contracts. A 1998 FBI videotape documented Freitas giving a $1,000 bribe to top Cianci aide Frank Corrente, whom the prosecution painted as Cianci's bag man and chief lieutenant.

The Plunder Dome investigation became public in 1999 when the FBI raided City Hall and arrested two top tax officials, David Ead and Joseph Pannone. Ead later testified against Cianci, who was indicted in 2001 on racketeering and conspiracy charges. Cianci, Frank Corrente and tow truck owner and businessman Richard Autiello were convicted in a 2002 trial.

Cianci reported to prison in New Jersey in December 2002, emerging in May 2007 slimmer and without his toupee. He returned to talk radio in Providence, taking great delight in castigating Providence mayor David Cicilline. Cicilline had his own problems with the tax collector's office, and his staff was accused by one tax official of improper influence on behalf of the Mayor's brother, lawyer John Cicilline, who, at the time the story broke, was imprisoned on another matter. Cicilline eventually fired the disgruntled tax collector (a hold-over from the Cianci days) for poor performance.

TAKE5 FIVE JAILED RHODE ISLAND PUBLIC FIGURES

1. **Buddy Cianci, Mayor of Providence**. Cianci pleaded guilty to assaulting Raymond DeLeo with an ashtray, fireplace log and lit cigarette in 1983. Cianci had invited DeLeo, whom he suspected of sleeping with his ex-wife, to his house and kept him prisoner for several hours. Cianci was given a five-year suspended sentence and resigned his post as mayor. Nearly two decades later, he was convicted in the Operation Plunder Dome investigation and sentenced to five years in prison.

2. **Edmund DiPrete, Governor of Rhode Island.** Ed DiPrete, who served as Rhode Island governor from 1985 to 1991, pleaded guilty in 1998 to multiple counts of extortion, embezzlement and bribery. A former Cranston mayor, DiPrete was brought down for showering political donors with government contracts. Among the more spectacular allegations during his trial was that DiPrete dove into a Walt's Roast Beef Dumpster on Reservoir Avenue in Cranston when a $10,000 bribe he had received was thrown out with a sandwich wrapper. DiPrete proclaimed his innocence of the charges, which had at one point been dismissed for prosecutorial misconduct, but accepted a plea deal and spent nearly a year at the ACI.

3. **Brian Sarault, Pawtucket Mayor**. Sarault took bribes in exchange for city contracts. He pleaded guilty to racketeering and extortion charges in 1991, and served four and a half years in federal prison.

4. **Anthony Almeida, Superior Court Judge**. Almeida pleaded guilty to accepting $45,000 in bribes from a lawyer in 1992, and was sent to prison for six years. Another judge who got into trouble was Joseph A. Bevilacqua, a Chief Justice of the Rhode Island Supreme Court in the 1980s. Bevilacqua was never criminally tried, but was censured and suspended for his social ties to organized crime figures, and his use of a mob-owned motel to conduct extra marital affairs.

5. **John Celona, State Senator, and Gerard Martineau, House Majority Leader**. The two state legislators were investigated under the auspices of the Operation Dollar Bill corruption probe and sent to prison in 2007 and 2008 for selling their services as public servants.

ultimately killed off the Connecticut coast.

Privateering was common throughout the eighteenth century, particularly during the Revolutionary period when there was either no national navy, or an underequipped and poorly staffed Continental Navy with which to defend the colonies. Privateering is ethically murky, as while technically privateers only attack enemy ships, this distinction was not always observed. Moreover, there was much flag switching among vessels and confusion about who owned what ship.

One of the most famous pirate/privateers of the 1600s was the Scot Captain William Kidd who was based in New York and active in the Caribbean, the Indian Ocean and the Americas. Kidd was hanged in London in 1701, but before meeting this fate he buried treasure in several places. One of these was Long Island, but he allegedly also secreted valuables on Block Island as well as Conanicut Island in Narragansett Bay. The Long Island treasure was soon found, but the Rhode Island loot, if it existed at all, is still unaccounted for.

Piracy has not always been frowned upon by government, and Samuel Cranston, who was Rhode Island governor from 1698-1727, had cordial relations with pirates. Piracy had its upside for the colony in that stolen goods were cheaper than those imported legally, and pirates had gold and silver to spend in the local economy. However, as the colony developed, piracy became a liability to trade and a threat to Rhode Island's shipping industry. The government decided to put a stop to it; the turning point was 1723 when 26 pirates were hanged en masse in Newport Harbor.

A DANCING COP AND A TV JUDGE

Tony Lepore (the Dancing Cop) and Judge Frank Caprio are well known to Rhode Island motorists. Lepore, a native of Providence's Silver Lake area, started his dancing routine in 1984 while directing traffic for the Providence Police Department. Before long, Lepore's spins and pirouettes resulted in appearances on *The Today Show* and *Good Morning America*, as well as coverage in international media. The mustachioed Lepore retired from the PPD in the late 1980s, but has

TAKE 5 FIVE SUBURBAN SLAYINGS

1. **Dr. Hani Zaki's murder, East Side of Providence, 2001**. Hani Zaki, a Providence doctor, was found dead by his mother-in-law, a bullet lodged in the back his head. Zaki was lying on the bed in the master bedroom of the expansive house he shared with his wife and children. Zaki had a number of mistresses, as well as questionable business associates. His wife was widely suspected of the still unsolved murder, but was never charged.

2. **Robert Sabetta Junior's assassination of three teenagers, Foster, 1993**. Foster police officer Sabetta shot four teenagers in an auto repair garage, killing three of them. At the time of the shooting, Sabetta was on suspension, the result of an assault charge brought against him by one of his teenaged victims

3. **The Brendel Family killings, Barrington, 1991**. Christopher J. Hightower, a Sunday school teacher and investment broker, killed his client Ernest Brendel with a crossbow, and then murdered Brendel's wife and the couple's eight-year-old daughter. Brendel had filed an investment fraud complaint against Hightower, who claimed at trial that the murders were committed by a gang of Asian drug traffickers who then forced him to bury the bodies.

4. **Teenaged killer Craig Price, Warwick, 1987 and 1989**. Fifteen-year-old Price was confronted by Joan Heaton and her two daughters, ages eight and 10, while robbing their house in the peaceful Buttonwoods area. He stabbed them dozens of times with a butcher knife. When Price was questioned in connection with the murders, he confessed, and further admitted to killing neighbor Rebecca Spencer two years earlier.

5. **Child killer Michael Woodmansee, South Kingstown, 1975**. Five-year-old Jason Foreman disappeared without a trace from out-side his house where he had been playing. The case remained unsolved until 1982 when a skull and bones were found in the bed-room of Michael Woodmansee, a 23-year-old neighbor well known for his involvement in community theater. Woodmansee had stabbed Foreman and hid the body in a trunk. He subsequently disposed of much of Foreman's remains, but kept some of the bones.

parlayed what was initially a means of livening up traffic duty into a mini empire. He stars in two cable television programs: *Safe Kids and Friends* (a safety show for children), and *On the Road with Tony the Dancing Cop*. Lepore also appears in parades and at festivals, and does corporate events, birthday parties, commercials and even the odd theatrical turn.

Judge Frank Caprio doesn't get the chance to bust a move during his gig, but he is a commanding presence nonetheless. Caprio grew up on Federal Hill, a milkman's son, and is now Chief Judge of the Providence Municipal Court. He is also the star of *Caught in Providence*, a cable show in which parking ticket scofflaws, red-light runners and a few misdemeanor offenders come before him to plead their cases. Caprio is generally receptive to a sob story from a sympathetic defendant, and often waives a fine or at least knocks it down, but there is no conning the avuncular judge, and he will deliver a pointed lecture, particularly to someone with a less than respectful attitude toward the court. When not in front of the camera or otherwise banging a gavel, Caprio is a partner in a Providence law firm, and chairs the Board of Governors for Higher Education in Rhode Island, among other professional, civic and charitable duties.

THE SMOKE SHOP RAID

A nasty and violent confrontation took place in July 2003 over the right of Narragansett Indians to sell tax-free cigarettes on tribal land. Under a 1978 agreement with the state, the Narragansetts control 1,800 acres in Charlestown; however, when they opened a smoke shop in a trailer there, Governor Carcieri ordered it shut down. Two days later, 30 state troopers descended and executed a search warrant.

Tribal members resisted the State Police's incursion, and a melee erupted in which several were injured and eight people, including Chief Sachem Matthew Thomas, were arrested. Governor Carcieri argued that the Narragansetts were breaking the law, and that the troopers were obstructed in the course of performing their job. The

Operation Dollar Bill

Rhode Island wouldn't be Rhode Island without a federal corruption investigation, and hot on the heels of Plunder Dome came Dollar Bill. The inquiry into influence peddling at the State House in the early 2000s threatened to ensnare a wide swath of Rhode Island lawmakers, and a number of prominent politicians were investigated. In the end, it turned out not to be that big a deal, although it did result in the conviction of John Celona (Chair of the Senate Corporations Committee) for selling his services as an elected official, and also nailed House Majority leader Gerard Martineau on similar charges.

On the receiving end of favors dispensed by Celona and Martineau were big players in the Rhode Island healthcare and insurance fields. Executives of Woonsocket-based drugstore empire CVS Corporation were accused of stealing John Celona's honest services by hiring him as a consultant, and then urging him to "take a walk" on a bill related to pharmacy choice.

Despite Celona's conviction, the CVS officials implicated in the scheme were ultimately acquitted. The once gregarious Celona, who had hosted a cable access television show in which he sung the praises of his patrons, agreed to testify to his role in the affair in exchange for a reduced sentence, but made a poor witness and was of little help to the government case.

In addition to CVS, Celona was also linked to Roger Williams Medical Center (RWMC), whose former president and CEO, Robert Urciuoli, was found guilty of buying Celona's influence on legislation. Finally, Blue Cross Blue Shield of Rhode Island also was deemed to have had an improper relationship with Celona and House Majority Leader Martineau. Martineau's company obtained lucrative bag contracts from Blue Cross and CVS in exchange for influencing legislation.

Operation Dollar Bill did not expose strong arm tactics such as were employed at Providence City Hall, nor was there money in envelopes or other such seedy goings-on. The probe did, however, confirm the cozy relationship that exists between Rhode Island politicians and certain well-heeled enterprises who know that rewarding their "friends" on Smith Hill with contracts and consulting fees is well worth the influence it provides.

Narragansetts countered that they were within their rights to conduct business on sovereign tribal land, and were intimidated and brutalized over what was essentially a tax issue.

A criminal trial, which was held up for several years until the federal courts ruled that the State Police did have the authority to enforce Rhode Island law on Narragansett tribal land, resulted in four convictions on 17 counts brought by the government. Three tribe members, including Chief Sachem Matthew Thomas, were found guilty of charges including disorderly conduct and simple assault; none were sentenced to time in prison. Four tribe members were acquitted of all charges; charges against a juvenile had been dropped previously.

The Narragansett Tribe was vigorous in defending its members during the trial, and also went on the offensive, filing a civil rights suit against the State Police in 2006. The lawsuit was dismissed, a decision that was upheld by a federal appeals panel in September 2008. One of the Narragansett men also filed suit for damages arising from an ankle broken in the raid. He was awarded $301,000 by a federal jury, but the verdict was set aside and a new trial ordered in which the state prevailed in arguing that excessive force was not used.

Weblinks

Rhode Island State Police
www.risp.ri.gov
Recruitment, press releases, crime statistics, photo galleries, Rhode Island's Ten Most Wanted and more.

Politics

In Rhode Island, politics truly is local. Nobody is more than 40 minutes from the capital, and rubbing elbows at a May Breakfast, Little League game or grocery store with an elected official is commonplace. There are lots of politicians in the state; in addition to the Governor, Congressional delegation and numerous municipal office holders, the Rhode Island General Assembly counts 113 members. Unlike in larger states where legislators often keep a residence in the capital and in their home district, Rhode Island Assembly members are part-timers who commute to their State House gig.

It would be nice to say that the "lively experiment" inaugurated by Roger Williams is thriving, but Rhode Islanders are generally cynical about their elected leaders. Corruption probes are not isolated events, but seem to be conducted on a rolling basis and have snared everyone from small town officials to governors and big city mayors. Moreover, some view Rhode Island politics as a closed shop in which it is difficult for outsiders, newcomers and freethinkers to gain influence, even if they do manage to get elected. The same group of politicians periodically shuffles positions, and many races are uncontested. The citizenry, despite vociferous carping in the letters pages of the state's newspapers and on talk radio, keeps throwing the bums back in. Still, some Rhode Island politicians are viewed with real affection, and the state has produced a number of genuine statesmen.

POLITICAL ORIGINS

In the 1630s and 1640s, dissidents and religious exiles including Roger Williams, Anne Hutchinson, William Coddington and Samuel Gorton established present day Providence, Portsmouth, Newport and Warwick. The settlers were soon menaced by the Massachusetts, Plymouth, Connecticut and New Haven colonies, and in response, Williams traveled to England and secured a Rhode Island charter from Parliament in 1644. In 1663, a Royal Charter, granted by King Charles II, established "Rhode Island and Providence Plantations" and guaranteed freedom of religion. The Charter was to remain in force until the adoption of the State Constitution in 1842.

INDEPENDENCE

By the eighteenth century, Rhode Island had become a leading shipping center, making it sensitive to a series of import duties imposed by Britain in the mid-1700s to pay for its colonial wars with France. The British Navy's attempts to halt smuggling led Rhode Island Colonists to fire a cannon on a British war ship in Newport in 1764, burn a revenue sloop in 1769, and beat a customs collector in 1771. Then, in 1772, in their most famous act of rebellion, Rhode Islanders organized by John Brown burned the British ship *Gaspee* and shot its captain after the boat ran aground in Warwick while pursuing smugglers.

Spurred by economic self-interest and similar resistance efforts occurring around Boston, in 1774 Rhode Island became the first colony to call

Did you know. . .

that Rhode Island's four Electoral College votes in presidential elections represent ¾ of one percent of the US total of 538? Despite this puny total, based on its population of about one million people, Rhode Island is actually substantially overrepresented in the Electoral College.

They said it

"The political condition of Rhode Island is notorious, acknowledged and it is shameful."

**– Lincoln Steffens in his 1905 *McClure's Magazine*
article "Rhode Island: A State for Sale."**

for a Continental Congress to develop an American response to British rule. On May 4, 1776, now celebrated as Rhode Island Independence Day, the state's General Assembly renounced its allegiance to the King. Rhode Island's best known Revolutionary War hero was Warwick-born General Nathanael Greene, a close ally of George Washington. Greene led forces in various battles in the North, but was immortalized for his service as Commander of the Southern Department.

When the Revolutionary War ended, Rhode Island was wary of again coming under centralized authority, and so was resistant to join the United States. In 1790, however, three years after Delaware was the first to sign on to the new US Constitution, and with a guarantee of a Bill of Rights in place, Rhode Island became the last of the original thirteen colonies to ratify the Constitution.

Did you know. . .

that Providence-born John McLaughlin, acerbic host of the TV current affairs program *The McLaughlin Group*, ran as a Republican against Democrat John Pastore in the 1970 Rhode Island US Senate race? McLaughlin, who holds a Ph.D. in philosophy from Columbia University, was at that time a Catholic priest and ran on an anti Vietnam War platform. McLaughlin lost the Senate contest, but became a speech writer and confidante of Richard Nixon. McLaughlin ultimately left the priesthood under pressure from Church authorities who were displeased with his outspoken and politically partisan views.

TAKE 5 JENNIFER LAWLESS'S FIVE THINGS
WE *DON'T* HAVE IN RHODE ISLAND POLITICS

Jennifer L. Lawless, Ph.D., is the director of American University's Women & Politics Institute in Washington, DC. Lawless was previously an assistant professor of political science at Brown University. She is the author of the book *It Takes A Candidate: Why Women Don't Run for Office*, as well as numerous academic articles. In 2006, she sought the Democratic nomination for the US House of Representatives in Rhode Island's Second Congressional District. Lawless was defeated by incumbent James Langevin, but has continued to advocate for increasing the number of women holding elected office.

1. **A Two-Party System**. Following the 2008 elections, Rhode Island has fewer Republicans serving in the state legislature than any other state. With only six Republicans in the House and four in the Senate, Rhode Island's General Assembly is 91 percent Democratic — the highest proportion in the country. Coupled with the fact that the entire congressional delegation (two US Senators and two members of the House of Representatives) is Democratic, as are four of our five statewide elected officials, Rhode Island is the bluest state in the nation.

2. **Women**. Rhode Island may be the bluest of blue states. And we may have given George W. Bush his lowest approval rating in the country. Yet despite our progressive tendencies, our political system is an old boy's club. We've never had a female governor. We've never had a female US Senator. Only six women have ever held statewide office. We haven't had a woman in our congressional delegation in eighteen years. And fewer women served in the General Assembly in 2008 than did twenty years ago.

3. **Electoral Competition**. The media tend to focus on bitterly contested elections, like the 2006 US Senate election between Sheldon Whitehouse and Lincoln Chafee. But the reality is that Rhode Island has very limited electoral competition. Nearly 40 percent of the seats in the General Assembly went uncontested in the 2008 general election. Another 35 percent saw the winner receive at least 60 percent of the vote. And 2008 was not an anomaly; this is how Rhode Island's political landscape tends to look.

4. **Traditionally Catholic Views**. Rhode Island is the most Catholic state in the nation; indeed, 61 percent of the population identifies that way. But when it comes to social policy, Rhode Islanders embrace a separation of church and state. That is, they are far more progressive than we might expect. Survey data indicates that roughly 65 percent of Rhode Islanders consider themselves pro-choice. Nearly two-thirds favored legalizing marijuana for medicinal purposes. And more than 40 percent support granting marriage rights to same-sex couples.

5. **County Government**. Rhode Island is one of only two states without an operational county government. Our state is divided into five counties, but these geographic barriers have no political meaning. Instead, the 39 municipalities throughout the state each have their own local government. This might not seem particularly relevant, but critics argue that in times of fiscal constraints, budget shortfalls, and dwindling resources, operating so many local units comes at the expense of spending on education, social services, and infrastructure.

THE DORR WAR AND THE FIGHT FOR POPULAR CONTROL

In the 1820s and 1830s, populist Jacksonian democracy dominated the nation, but Rhode Island's voting laws remained restrictive. An influx of landless Irish immigrants, coupled with property requirements, meant that by 1840 only one third of white males could vote. Moreover, the apportionment system favored rural areas, and didn't account for changing city sizes. Newport had more seats than Providence, despite having only 40 percent of the latter's population. These factors led urban whites to rebel in what would be known as the "Dorr War."

Thomas Wilson Dorr, a Harvard-educated lawyer, had pushed for expanded suffrage in the 1830s as a member of the General Assembly. In 1841, Dorr and his allies pressured the legislature to call a constitutional convention, but when the legislature declared that only property owners could elect delegates, the Dorr forces organized their own "People's Convention." A "People's Constitution" expanded suffrage and granted urban areas greater representation. The People's party held elections under its newly drafted constitution, electing Dorr governor.

Meanwhile, the General Assembly Landholders elected Samuel King governor. King ordered Dorr's arrest, but the reformer fled to Washington, DC where he unsuccessfully sought the support of President John Tyler. Dorr returned to Providence on May 17, 1842, and with two cannons and 234 supporters, attempted to seize the Providence Armory. The cannons failed to fire, militia men rushed to defend the armory, and the rebellion fizzled in the fog. Dorr and his supporters repaired to Glocester, but 2,500 government troops descended and arrested over 100. Dorr escaped to Connecticut, but was returned to Rhode Island and imprisoned. He was given a life sentence, but served only a year due to ill health and died in 1845.

Dorr's fight was not in vain. In December 1842, another convention was called; it gave black men equal voting rights, and increased representation for northern cities. However, the Dorr Rebellion was the beginning, not the end, of the fight for popular control. A number of exclusionary features remained, including poll taxes for landless US-born voters, and prohibitions on foreign-born citizens voting. Over time, these and other inequities were remedied, including granting women the vote in 1917.

GOVERNOR GREEN AND "THE BLOODLESS REVOLUTION"

The 1934 election of Governor Theodore Francis Green enabled the Democrats to seize control of state government, ending Republican dominance in Rhode Island state politics. Green challenged the election of two Republican state senators, and in a rapid series of moves, replaced the five-member Republican Supreme Court with new justices to insure Republican recount appeals would fail.

The "revolution" also transferred key appointments from the state Senate to the governor, set minimum wages for women and children, created unemployment compensation and established a 48-hour work week. The Democrats have controlled the Rhode Island House of Representatives since 1934.

Untouched by Green's moves was an apportionment system that gave each town at least one state senator. This formula favored rural areas, and allowed Republicans to control the Senate until as late as 1958. Despite their generally lackluster numbers in the General Assembly, Republicans often win the governorship, usually after a hotly-contested primary divides the Democratic Party. The Republican Governor then must work with a heavily Democratic General Assembly that is able to override a Governor's veto.

Did you know. . .

that from 1663 until 1854, Rhode Island had five capitals? Providence, Newport, East Greenwich, Bristol and South Kingstown all shared the role. In 1854, only Providence and Newport remained as capitals, and in 1900 Providence assumed sole possession of the title.

TAKE 5 TOP FIVE TITANS OF
TWENTIETH CENTURY RHODE ISLAND POLITICS

1. **Theodore Francis Green (1867-1966)**. Democrat Green was descended from Rhode Island's original settlers. Described by *Time* magazine as "The Boulevardier Brahmin," Green was a lifelong bachelor, fitness buff, bon vivant and gentleman scholar. He was also fabulously rich and has an airport named after him. Green served as governor of Rhode Island from 1933 to 1937, and was elected to the US Senate in 1937 when he was 69. He retired in 1961 at age 93.

2. **James Howard McGrath (1903-1966)**. Democrat McGrath was US District Attorney for Rhode Island from 1934 to 1940, and governor from 1940-45. He briefly served as US Solicitor General, and was a US senator from 1947 to 1949, resigning his post to become Attorney General. McGrath had chaired the Democratic National Committee, but ultimately had to resign as AG for failing to cooperate with a 1950s investigation at the Department of Justice.

3. **John O. Pastore (1907-2000)**. Democrat Pastore was governor from 1945-1950, and was known for his liberal views, skill as an orator and short stature – he stood five feet four inches. Pastore was elected to the US Senate in 1950, and served for 26 years. He played an important role in the passage of the 1964 Civil Rights Act, and chaired the Joint Committee on Atomic Energy.

4. **Claiborne Pell (1918-2009)**. Democrat Pell was in the US Senate from 1961-1997. Prior to becoming a senator, Pell served on behalf of the Foreign Service and State Department, and participated in the conference that established the UN. Pell was known for his efforts to make higher education accessible, and the Pell Grants are named in his honor. Pell was also the principal sponsor of the 1965 law that established the National Endowment for the Arts and the National Endowment for the Humanities.

5. **John Chafee (1922-1999)**. Republican Chafee was governor of Rhode Island from 1963-1969. He was Secretary of the Navy under Richard Nixon from 1969-1972, and served in the US Senate from 1976 until his 1999 death in office. A moderate Republican, Chafee was a champion of environmental causes and chaired the Senate Environment and Public Works Committee.

WOMEN IN RHODE ISLAND POLITICS
- First woman to serve in the Rhode Island House of Representatives: Isabelle Ahearn O'Neill, elected 1922, Democrat, Providence.
- First woman to serve in the Rhode Island Senate: Lulu Mowry Schlesinger, elected 1928, Republican, Charlestown.
- First woman appointed to the Rhode Island Supreme Court: Florence Murray, 1979.
- First and only woman to serve as Rhode Island Attorney General: Arlene Violet, elected 1984, Republican.
- First and only woman elected Senate President: Teresa Paiva-Weed, 2009. Paiva-Weed, a Democrat from Newport-Jamestown, was first elected to the House in 1992 and also became the first female Senate Majority Leader in 2004.
- First and only woman to serve as Rhode Island Lieutenant Governor: Elizabeth Roberts, elected 2006, Democrat.
- First and only Rhode Island woman elected to the US Congress: Claudine Schneider, elected to the first of five terms, 1980, Republican, Second Congressional District.

GOVERNOR PRIMER
- Youngest elected governor: William Sprague II (30 in 1860)
- Oldest elected governor: James Fenner (72 in 1843)
- Longest-serving governor since statehood: Arthur Fenner (1790-1805)
- First governor elected to a four-year term: Lincoln Almond (1994) (Governors previously served two-year terms)
- Number of governors who have resigned to become United States Senators: 4
- Last governor to resign to become United States Senator: John Pastore (1950)

They said it

THE CURRENT STATE GOVERNMENT

- Governor: Donald Carcieri, Republican (first elected 2002)
- Lieutenant Governor: Elizabeth Roberts, Democrat (elected 2006)
- Secretary of State: Ralph Mollis, Democrat (elected 2006)
- House Speaker: William Murphy, Democrat (first elected to post in 2003)
- Senate President: Teresa Paiva-Weed, Democrat (elected to post in 2009)
- Number of State Senators: 38
- Number of State House Representatives: 75
- State Senate composition: Democrats 33, Republicans 4, Independent 1
- State House of Representatives composition: Democrats 69, Republicans 6
- Number of women legislators (both chambers): 25
- Ratio of state legislators to state residents: 1 for every 9,448 Rhode Islanders

Did you know...

that Rhode Island is the most Democratic state in the nation? According to a Gallup poll, the Rhode Island gap between Democrat and Republican support is 37 percentage points. Massachusetts and Hawaii are close behind at 34 points, and Vermont has a gap of 33 points. The most Republican state is Utah where the Republicans hold a 23 point advantage over the Democrats.

CONGRESSIONAL DELEGATION

- Senator Jack Reed, Democrat. First elected in 1996 (preceded by Democrat Claiborne Pell).
- Senator Sheldon Whitehouse, Democrat. Elected in 2006 (preceded by Republican Lincoln Chafee).
- Congressman Patrick Kennedy, Democrat. 1st Congressional District, first elected 1994 (preceded by Republican Ronald Machtley).
- Congressman James Langevin, Democrat. 2nd Congressional District, first elected 2000, (preceded by Democrat Bob Weygand).

TAKE5 TOP FIVE RHODE ISLAND
STATEHOUSE FACTS

1. The 11-foot tall statute of the Independent Man that stands atop the Statehouse dome has been hit by lightning 27 times. The 500-pound gold leaf covered figure was cast from the remains of a statute of Latin American liberator Simon Bolivar that once stood in New York City's Central Park.

2. The Rhode Island General Assembly moved into the building, which is constructed of 327,000 cubic feet of Georgia Marble and 15 million bricks, in 1901.

3. The House and Senate chambers are not air conditioned, making legislators sweat during June budget debates, regardless of the depth of the financial crisis unfolding.

4. In addition to the Royal Charter of 1663, other items on display in the State House include an original copy of the Declaration of Independence, a sliver of the moon, some sand from the Battle of Iwo Jima, a Civil War cannon and an 1802 portrait of George Washington by Rhode Island artist Gilbert Stuart.

5. The dome is the fourth largest self-supporting marble dome in the world, trailing only St. Peter's in Rome, the Minnesota State Capitol and the Taj Mahal.

Vincent "Buddy" Cianci

Rhode Island's best known rogue is former Providence Mayor Vincent "Buddy" Cianci who served three terms as mayor, resigned following a felony conviction, was reelected to three more terms, only to resign again after being convicted on federal corruption charges.

"Buddy," as he is universally known, was born in 1941 in Cranston and first elected Providence Mayor in 1974, defeating incumbent Democrat Joseph Doorley by 709 votes. The 32-year-old Cianci ran as a Republican on an anti-corruption platform, and won the strongly Democratic city in part thanks to a bitter four-way Democratic mayoral primary.

His first term was dominated by late budgets, public works strikes, and the 1978 suicide of the police chief. A police lieutenant publicly blamed the death on Cianci for having forced the chief to hire unqualified recruits. That year, *The New Times* magazine also reported that Cianci had raped a woman while a student at Marquette University Law School. Cianci admitted to spending the evening with the women and paying her $3,000 after she dropped her complaint, but sued the magazine for libel. He received an $8,500 settlement and an apology, handily winning reelection in the mean time.

In 1980, Cianci ran for governor but suffered a humiliating defeat, capturing only 26 percent of the vote. During his second mayoral term, he laid off city workers and fired the city's garbage collectors. Cianci hired a contractor to replace the sanitation men, and deployed shot-gun carrying police officers aboard the trucks to protect the new recruits. He remained a popular figure throughout the controversy.

Cianci was more than a politician, he was a star and a quick wit who made even the press and his opponents laugh. He narrowly won a third mayoral bid by 1074 votes, but a subsequent *Providence Journal* investigation determined that the election could have been decided by mail ballot fraud. Cianci's third term ended prematurely when he pleaded *nolo contendere* to two assault charges on his estranged wife's alleged lover. Cianci called Raymond DeLeo to his Providence East Side home and in the presence of a police officer and two other city officials, berated, spit upon, kicked and hit the man for more than two hours. Cianci also burned DeLeo with a lit cigarette and threatened to kill him if he did not pay him $500,000. DeLeo went to the State Police, and Cianci ultimately received a five-year suspended sentence, disqualifying him from serving as mayor. There were also ethics problems at City Hall in the early 1980s, and when corruption trials had finished, 22 former city officials had been convicted, although Cianci was not charged.

During what he later called his "sabbatical," Cianci remained prominent as a local radio talk show host. Cianci also rolled out the "Mayor's Own Marinara Sauce," which featured his picture on the label and benefitted Providence school children. One year after his sentence expired, Cianci announced he would run for mayor in 1990 as an independent. With his base of working class Italian-Americans, Cianci narrowly won a three-way race, the outcome again determined by mail ballots. In 1994 and 1998, he easily won reelection to fifth and sixth terms, becoming the face of the Providence Renaissance, which was the result of federal, state and city efforts to rebuild downtown Providence in the 1980s and 90s. Among other projects, the waste-land of rail tracks and parking lots near the State House was cleared to allow for a new train station, downtown rivers were uncovered and altered, and Waterplace Park created. Finally, big retail returned to downtown in the form of Providence Place Mall. The mayor campaigned relentlessly on these and other achievements; the joke went that he would attend the opening of an envelope.

Cianci's second mayoral stint ended in disgrace in 2002 when he was convicted of one RICO felony charge of conspiracy in a federal investigation into corruption at Providence City Hall. Cianci spent five years in a New Jersey prison, and then returned to Providence and took up work again as a radio talk show host, a position which seems as natural to him as his former one of mayor. The charismatic Cianci, who was the longest sitting mayor in Providence history, remains a polarizing figure, credited by some as the architect of Providence's resurgence and a true champion of the city, but derided by others as a bully and a throwback to earlier eras when patronage and back room deals trumped accountability and clean government.

Nelson Aldrich: The General Manager of the United States

Born in Foster in 1841 to a descendent of Roger Williams, Aldrich's great power resulted in his being dubbed "the General Manager of the United States." Aldrich served in the US Senate from 1881 to 1911, and as a member of the Senate Finance Committee, he opposed populist efforts to expand the money supply, and fought President Theodore Roosevelt's railroad regulation.

A true tycoon, Aldrich shrewdly balanced Hawaiian and Cuban sugar interests, making millions adjusting sugar tariffs and investing in the industry. At the end of his Senate career, he took the first steps in establishing the Federal Reserve System, although he wanted the system's board members elected by banks, not appointed by the President.

Locally, Aldrich teamed with political boss Charles Brayton, a former Chief of the Rhode Island State Police, to run Rhode Island's then powerful Republican Party machine. In the 1890s, Aldrich, Brayton and "Utility King" Marsden Perry ran roughshod over the state legislature, buying influence and crafting laws that allowed the trio to dominate the electricity and public transportation sectors. Lincoln Steffens's 1905 *McClure's Magazine* exposé of Rhode Island political corruption entitled "Rhode Island: A State for Sale," focused on the close union of Aldrich, Brayton and Perry's business interests, and laws enacted by the State Assembly.

Shortly after Brayton's 1910 death, Aldrich retired from the US Senate. His Benevolent Street home in Providence currently houses the Rhode Island Historical Society, while his Warwick Neck estate, once called the "house that sugar built," is owned by the Roman Catholic Church's Diocese of Providence. The Aldrich Mansion, as it is known, is frequently used for weddings and corporate events. Nelson Aldrich's grandson, Nelson Aldrich Rockefeller, served as Governor of New York, and then United States Vice President during the 1960s and 1970s.

They said it

"I love Rhode Island. But civic life is a mockery. It always seems like amateur hour around here. Someday, I almost expect, Congress will intercede and announce it is yanking Rhode Island's license to be a state, half the residents will be designated citizens of Massachusetts and half assigned to Connecticut, and the flag will now have 49 stars, instead of 50."

– Longtime *Providence Journal* political columnist M. Charles Bakst in his September 15, 2008 farewell column.

2008 PRESIDENTIAL ELECTION RESULTS

Barack Obama (D): 63.1 percent
John McCain (R): 35.2 percent
Ralph Nader (I): 1.0 percent
Total votes cast: 475,000+
Eligible voters: 701,000+
Turnout: 67.8

Source: State of Rhode Island.

Did you know. . .

that Rhode Island's first openly gay or lesbian state official was state Senator William Fitzpatrick (D-Cranston), an Irish immigrant who served for two terms starting in 1993? Current gay Rhode Island politicians include Providence mayor David Cicilline, and Representative Gordon Fox (D-Providence, District 4) who is House Majority Leader in the Rhode Island House of Representatives.

TAKE 5 BRUCE SUNDLUN'S TOP FIVE
ACHIEVEMENTS AS GOVERNOR

Bruce Sundlun is Governor-in-Residence and teaches political science at URI. Sundlun was born in 1920 in Providence, and grew up on the city's East Side. He graduated from Williams College, and then served as a bomber pilot in WWII, where he narrowly escaped capture by the Nazis when he parachuted out of his damaged B-17 into farm country in occupied Belgium. He evaded capture for six months before entering Switzerland, where he worked for the Office of Strategic Services. Following the war, Sundlun attended Harvard Law and served in the Justice Department in Washington. He later headed Rhode Island's The Outlet Company, which he transformed into a profitable communications corporation. Sundlun served as Governor of Rhode Island from 1990-94.

1. **Closing the Banks**. I was inaugurated on January 1st, but the previous night, while on my way to a party, I was presented a one-sentence letter: "At 5:00 pm today the Board of Governors of the Rhode Island Share and Deposit Corporation voted unanimously to put the company into conservatorship, because of a lack of cash." I called State Police Superintendant Colonel Edmond Culhane and asked that he put a state trooper on every credit union in the state. I wasn't worried about depositors raiding the banks, but thought credit union officials might take the books. The Colonel agreed, and their logs showed 36 attempts to remove records. The next day, two hours after my inauguration, I closed all of the state's banks and credit unions. Twenty-three of them never reopened, but within two-and-a-half years, all the depositors were repaid, with interest.

2. **Confronting the Biggest Deficit in State History**. The second day of my administration, I learned Rhode Island had a $265 million deficit. Governor Edward DiPrete, my predecessor, had sworn on television that there was no deficit. I met with Harry Baird, Director of the Department of Administration, and legislative leaders and we decided to ask employees to defer 12.5 percent of their pay for the balance of the year, and the following one, and that we also lay off 650 employees. State Senate President John Bevilacqua said, "Governor, I have great respect for you, but Democrats do not lay off people." I called Baird, "Get rid of the

lay offs, and increase the percentage to compensate." We agreed on 14.5 percent, and I learned a lesson about governing.

3. **Payless Payday**. The morning of my third day in office, I was told, "We're going to have a payless payday on February 20th." In order to avert this, I asked Harry Baird how much we spent weekly on payroll; he replied, "About $2.1 million." I told him that we needed to save that amount by taking a percentage of it from employees' checks each pay period, paying it back later with interest. The plan worked.

4. **Workers' Compensation Companies Threat**. On the fourth morning, my secretary informed me, "There are 12 presidents of workers' compensation insurance companies in the State Room. They don't have an appointment. They want a 123 percent increase in premiums, or else they'll stop offering workers compensation insurance." I asked the group to find a room and sit down while I discussed the matter with my staff. The Liberty Mutual President said, "Governor, there are 12 of us, and only one of you, and I suggest that it is easier for you to find a place to sit down than us." A vulgar answer arose in my throat, but I never stated it. I told my Executive Counsel Sheldon Whitehouse, "You've got two months to cure the defects in our workers' comp system." Sheldon created a 55-person committee composed of business, labor, academia and the Workers' Compensation Court. They drafted a bill, the legislature passed it unanimously, and today 35 states have copied Rhode Island's statute.

5. **No Corruption**. At the end of two terms, my administration had a perfect record -- no corruption or criminality. During the first week of the administration, I told all employees I was determined to have an honest government; if anyone of them were charged with corruption or violations of ethics laws, I would fire them that day! If they wanted to sue for their job, they could, and the state would defend the lawsuit. If the employee won, he/she could claim their job plus damages. The state would give them a job in a nice abandoned building in the Chepachet Woods. Three-hundred-fifty state employees on worker's comp came back to work, all claiming that their health had recovered.

They said it

PREVIOUS RHODE ISLAND PRESIDENTIAL VOTE WINNERS (NATIONAL WINNER IN PARENTHESES):

- 2004: John Kerry (D) (George W. Bush)
- 2000: Al Gore (D) (George W. Bush)
- 1996: Bill Clinton (D) (Bill Clinton)
- 1992: Bill Clinton (D) (Bill Clinton)
- 1988: George H. W. Bush (R) (George H. W. Bush)
- 1984: Ronald Reagan (R) (Ronald Reagan)
- 1980: Jimmy Carter (D) (Ronald Reagan)
- 1976: Jimmy Carter (D) (Jimmy Carter)
- 1972: Richard Nixon (R) (Richard Nixon)
- 1968: Hubert Humphrey (D) (Richard Nixon)

Did you know...

that during his eight years in office, President G.W. Bush visited Rhode Island only once? Bush's sole trip to the Ocean State was a brief June 2007 Newport jaunt in which he toured the area by helicopter and then spoke on the subject of terrorism at Newport Naval War College.